THEMATIC CHESS TRAINING 10

ANTONIO GUDE

MATE

COMBINATIONS

128 THEMATIC EXERCISES FOR STRUCTURED TRAINING

EDITORA

SOLIS

2023

© Antonio Gude 2004
© 2023 of the English edition by Garcez Leme & Associados, Lda.
Editors: Francisco Garcez Leme and Jussara Chaves Garcez Leme
Layout: Heloísa Chaves Garcez Leme
Published in Aveiro, Portugal in 2023
ISBN: 9786598628130

SUMMARY   PAGE

INTRODUCTION

Theory establishes didactic models in the treatment of positions, or in the study of different technical themes, but practice is responsible for creating chaos with its diversity, which is precisely one of the great attractions of chess.

The *Chess School* manuals (1 and 2) have a strong practical orientation, as shown by the fact that, in addition to the numerous positions commented on in the main body, both books contain an additional block of 160 and 128 exercises, respectively.

Nevertheless, the effort to systematize the material, reducing it to valid models, for the sake of the best possible didactic orientation, is not enough for the player to grasp the variety and richness of competitive chess.
This editorial initiative responds to the active player's need to cultivate systematic training, and these books, with 128 exercises each, at three levels of difficulty, will contribute to solving this aspect, because they are theme parks, with positions that expand on monographic aspects developed theoretically in the manuals.

Each book is divided into sections, and the exercises in these sections are rated with one, two or three stars, according to the degree of difficulty, in line with the technique used in *Chess School* (1 and 2).
Measuring the difficulty of an exercise is not easy. Not just because the objective assessment is difficult in itself, but because the degree of difficulty is different for each person. The aim of these books is to reach as many chess players as possible, because that is the only way to justify their publication. In general terms, I believe that the resolution time should be:

First level	★	(1 star)	1- 3 minutes
Second level	★★	(2 stars)	5 -10 minutes
Third level	★★★	(3 stars)	10 -20 minutes

There's no need to be too strict about the reflection time. Self-taught players can be guided by this estimate, while - as we suggested in *Chess School* - the ideal is for the coach to set the exact amount of time for each exercise or block of exercises for a group of players or a specific player.

MATE COMBINATIONS

A combination has been defined in various ways. Perhaps the best known is that it is a forced sequence of moves, with sacrifice(s). It should be noted that these moves are usually spectacular and often unpredictable. The aim of any combination is to obtain a material or positional advantage, or a draw in the case of apparently lost positions. In this book, and when dealing with mate combinations, it is clear that the objective is the king.

Mate combinations were studied in *Chess School* (chapters 5 and 7), and especially in *Mate Combination Technique*, the first volume of the Encyclopedia of Tactics, as it is the book's monographic object of study.

In this book I've tried to offer the best mate combinations of the last eight years.

Only one formula is known for progressing in chess: play as many games as possible, together with theoretical study and analysis of the games themselves. The ideal complement to this formula is, as many great masters recommend, for the player to develop and perfect their tactical and strategic skills by solving numerous exercises, specially selected for their usefulness. Like the ones we offer here

1 - Rook Sacrifices

1 - Black plays  ★

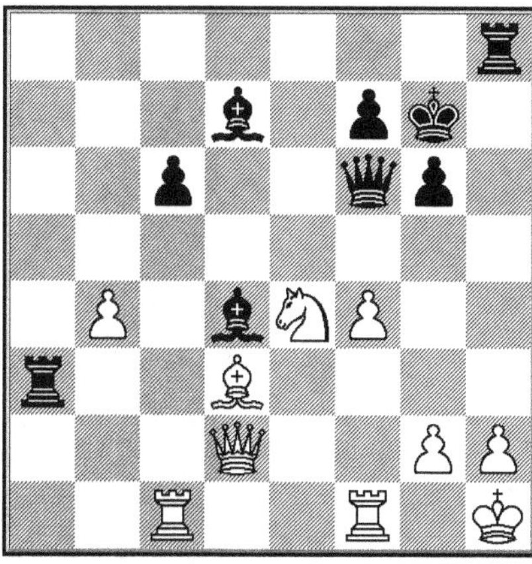

They're two top-notch players, but the finishing, dear Watson, is elementary (quick chess stuff).

3 - White plays  ★

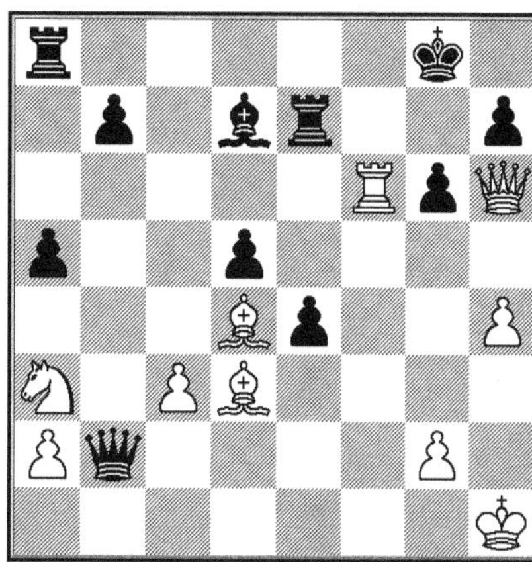

Black was hoping to win back a piece, gaining material, but the squares of his color around the King were making water.

2 - Black plays  ★

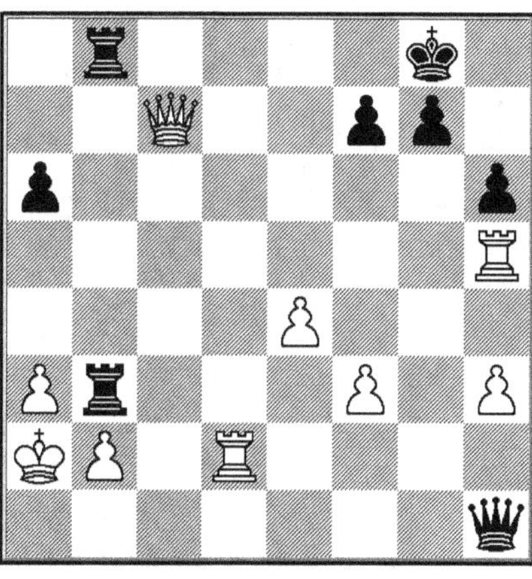

White made a very serious mistake in his last move (**29.♕c3–c7??**), which Black will now punish. How?

4 - White plays  ★

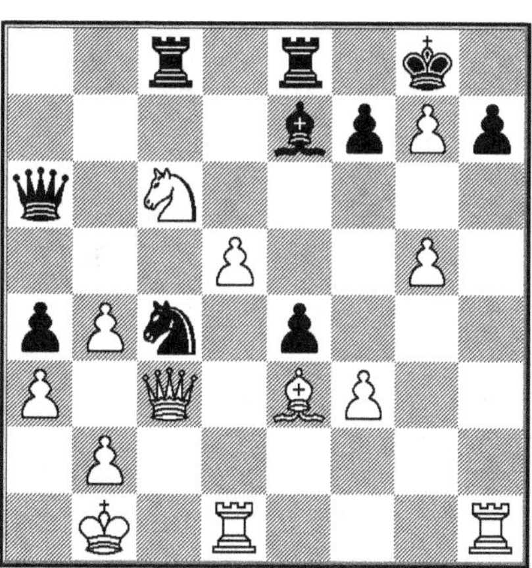

Everything is in place for the Whites to win quickly. In what way?

1 - Rook Sacrifices

5 - Black plays ★

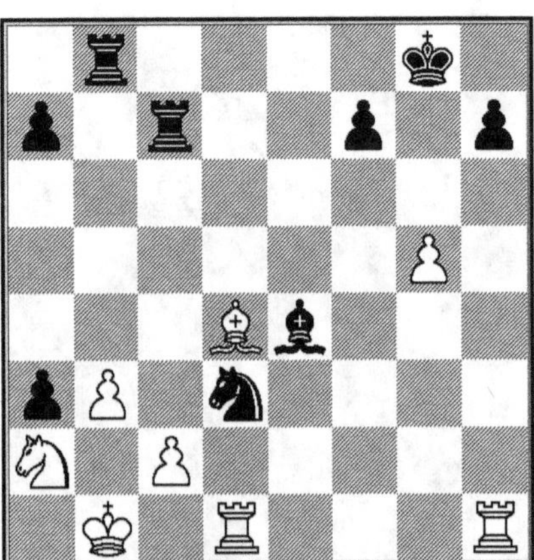

It's clear that Black has a decisive advantage, but he's not being asked to win, but to give mate in a few moves.

7 - Black plays ★★

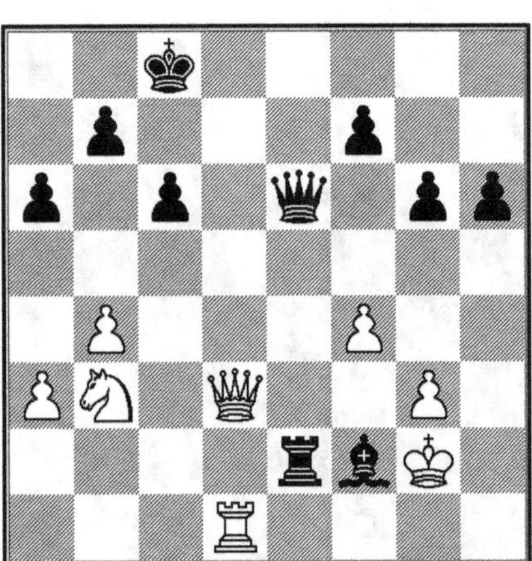

Like a ray of hope, White threatens an illusory mate on **d8**. How to finish?

6 - White plays ★

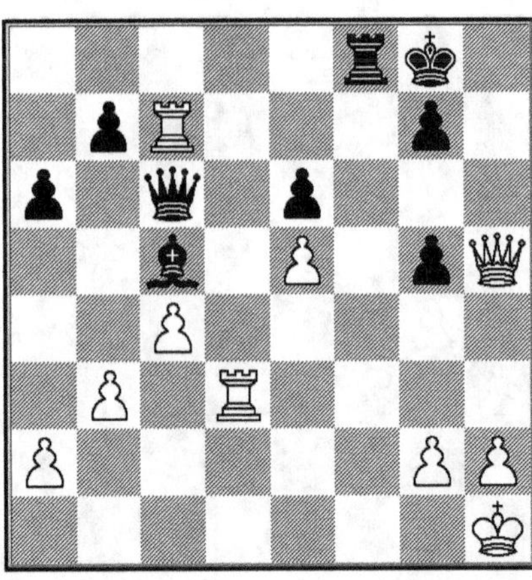

With **26...♖e8–f8** Black ignored the attack on his Queen, but this is not enough to save them.

8 - White plays ★★

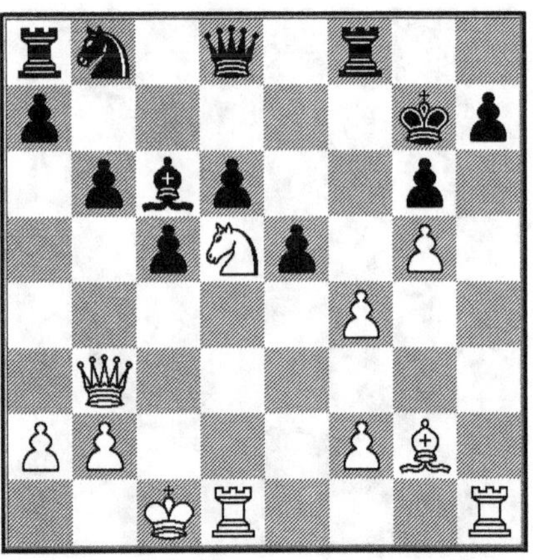

h-column and black squares are the main factors that lead to aggression. What would you do?

1 - Rook Sacrifices

9 - White plays 

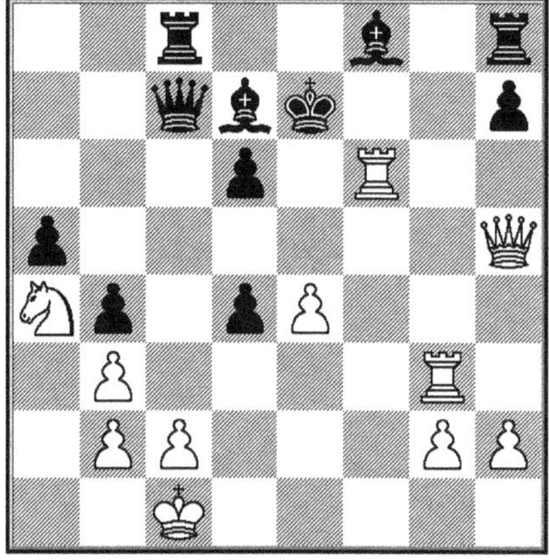

Seeing that touch of class that characterizes her at critical moments...

11 - White plays 

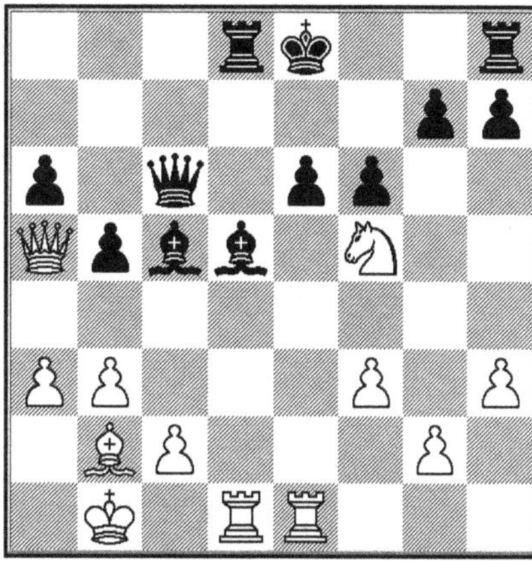

Another King in the center who will have problems getting away with it, although he's only one move away from happiness.

10 - White plays 

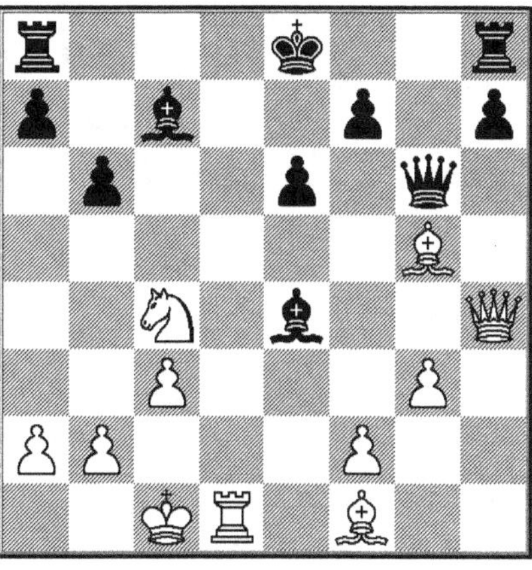

Castling has existed since the 16th century, but some players seem to ignore it. Black's King will succumb without exercising this right.

12 - White plays 

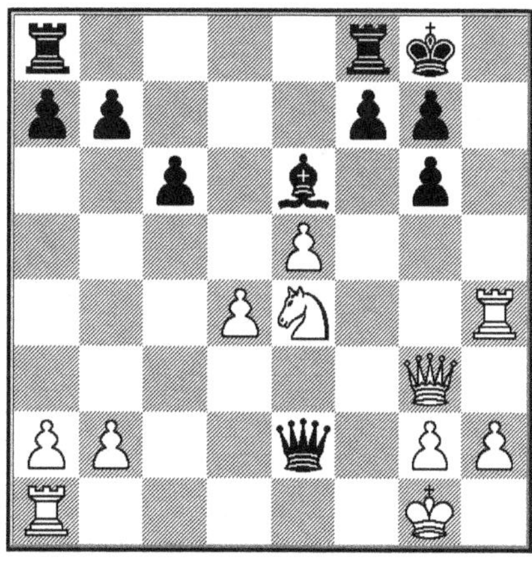

Black's Queen incurtion is doomed to failure, as White has a clear path on the h column. So...

1 - Rook Sacrifices

13 - White plays ★★★

White has an advantage in development and Black has weakened his castling with the ...h5 advance. Conclusion?

15 - White plays ★★★

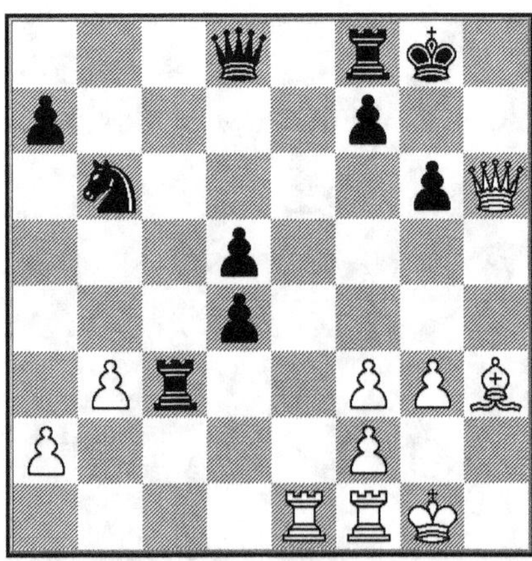

White has access to Black's King. How can they exploit their assets?

14 - White plays ★★★

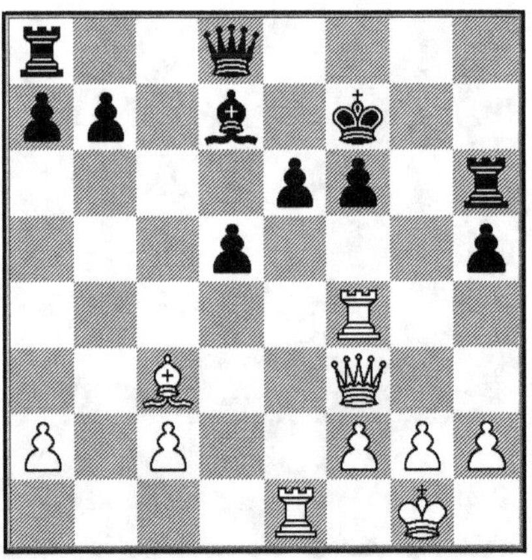

There are holes near Black's King and Bishops of opposite colors is a factor that favors the attacker. Any ideas?

16 - White plays ★★★

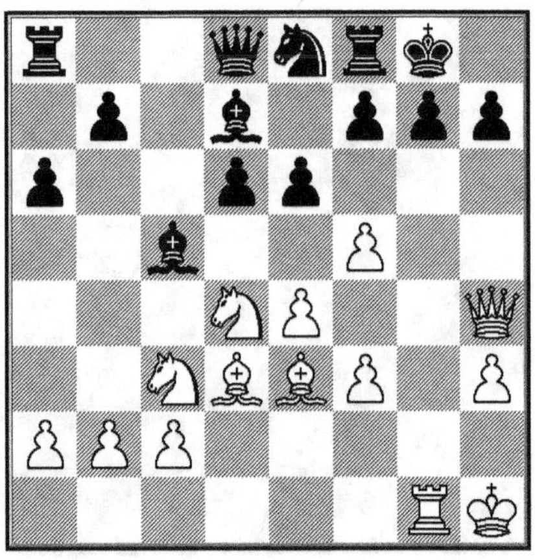

White has sacrificed a quality to open up the g column and is now ready to continue his attack. How?

2 - Smaler Piece Sacrifices

17 - Black plays 

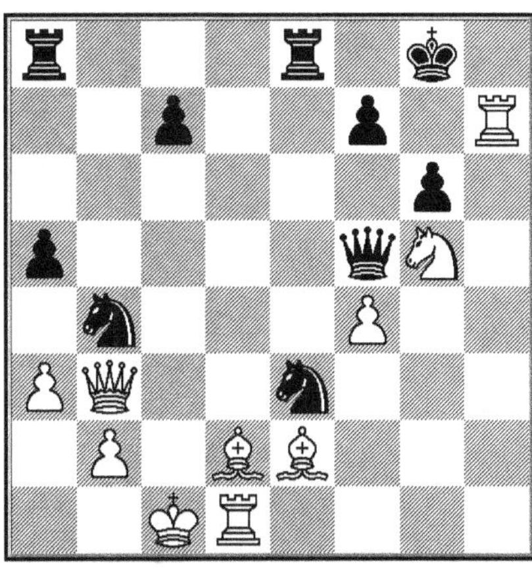

Incredibly, an elite Grandmaster has just played **26.♕b3??**, allowing for a comical endgame. Which one?

19 - White plays 

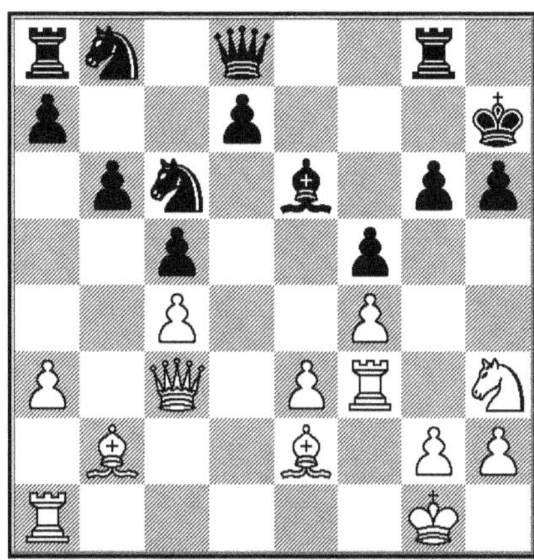

The position is ripe and ready for judgment. All you have to do is finish.

18 - White plays 

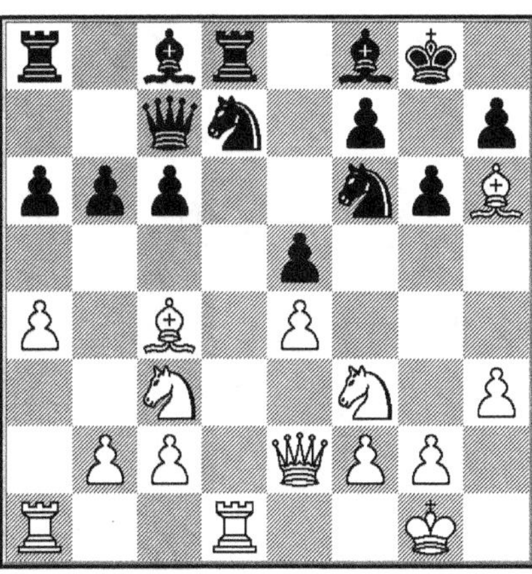

Black has made an opening blunder, which his opponent is in a position to exploit immediately. How?

20 - Black plays 

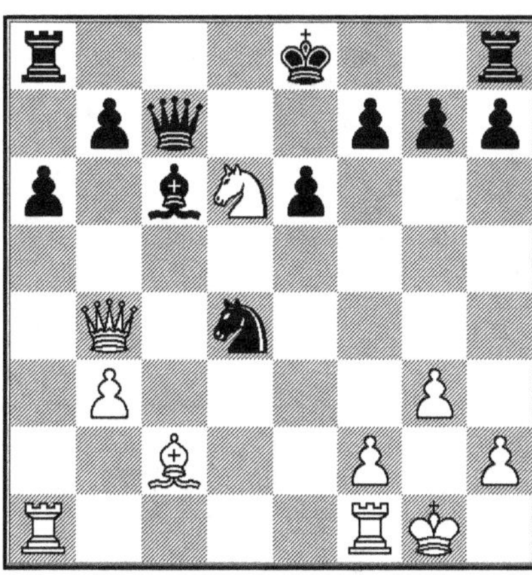

A very strong check at first glance. But haven't White forgotten something?

2 - Smaler Piece Sacrifices

21 - Black plays ★★

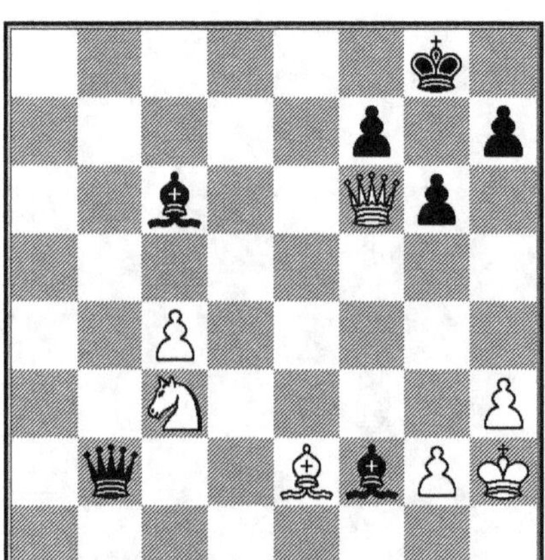

Too easy? Well, the victim was a Grand Master with 2689 Elo!

23 - Black plays ★★

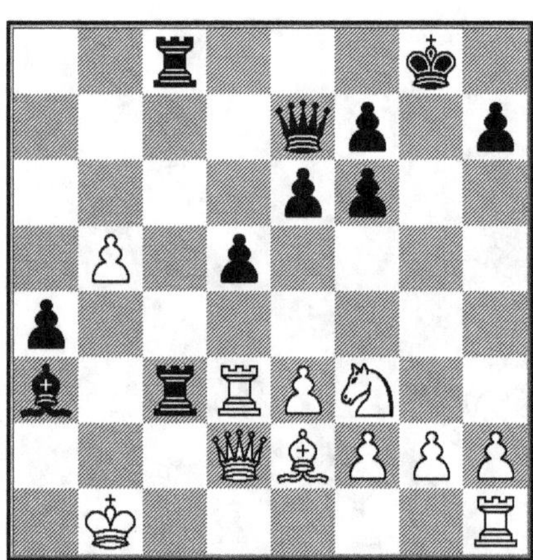

The black pieces occupy optimal invasion positions, which justifies the sacrificed piece. Emule Short.

22 - White plays ★★

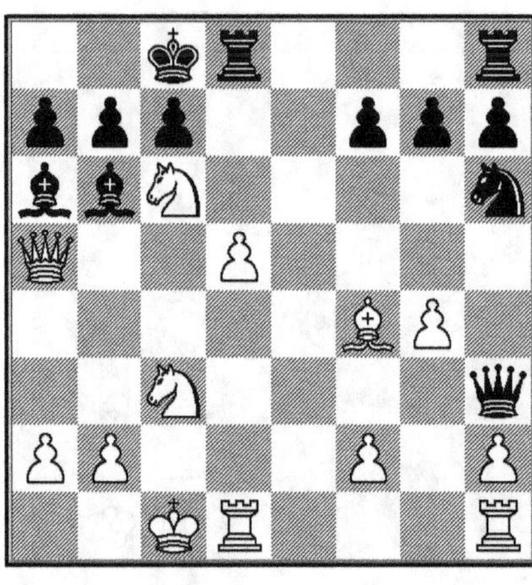

In fact, what we have here is a *pseudo-combination*. But it will serve as a calculation exercise. Run it.

24 - White plays ★★

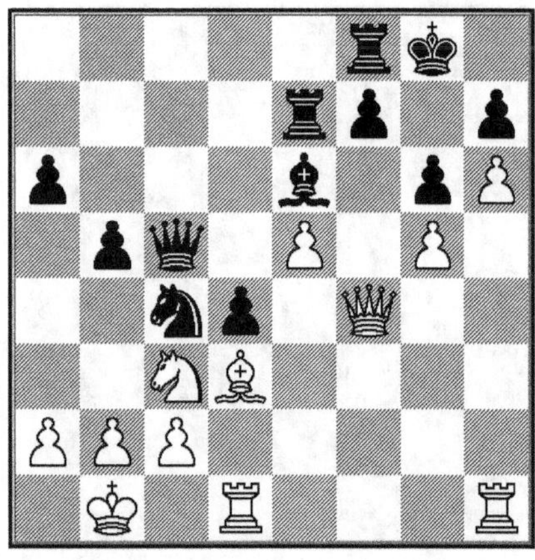

The Queen's entry on f6 is no good, as ...♛×e5. But the theme is too strong to ignore...

2 - Smaler Piece Sacrifices

25 - White plays  ★ ★

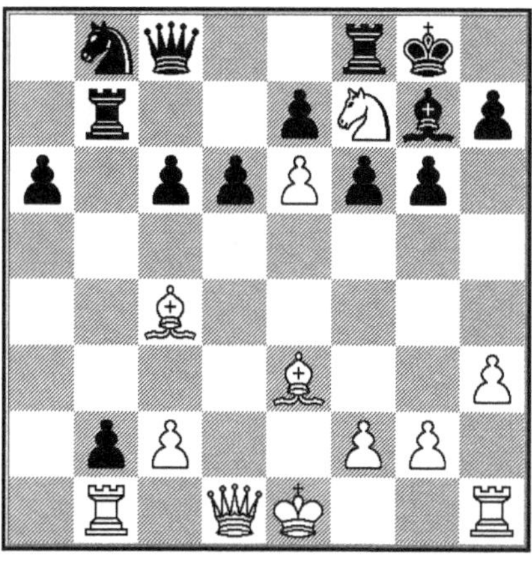

The Knight and pawn embedded in the enemy camp are the emissaries of the apocalypse. What will you do?

27 - White plays  ★ ★

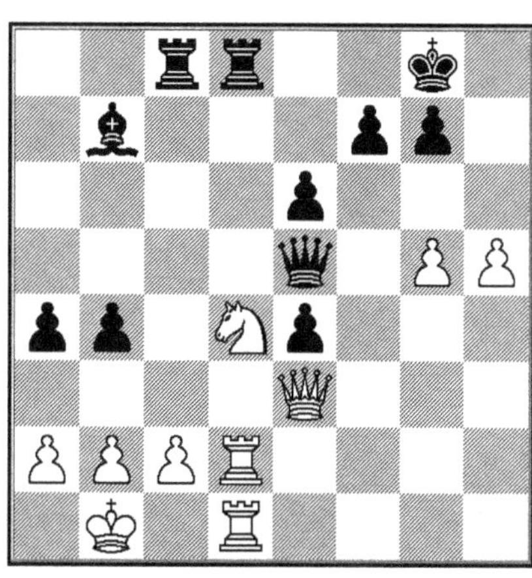

The typical mutual attacks with opposing castlings are in action. White arrives first.

26 - Black plays  ★ ★

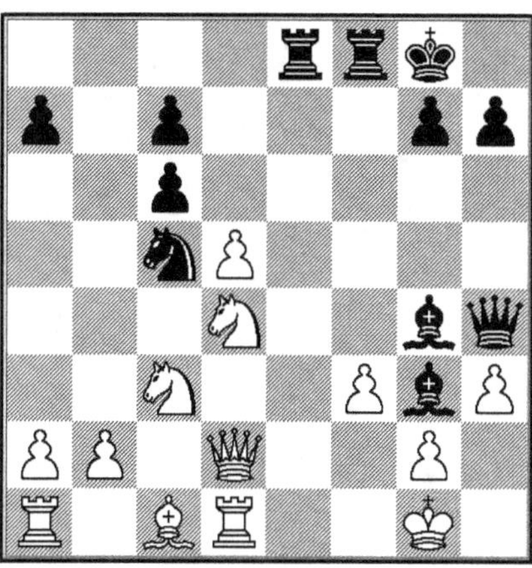

White's castling is very weak and although it has a Bishop of black squares, it's buried in its starting square.

28 - Black plays  ★ ★

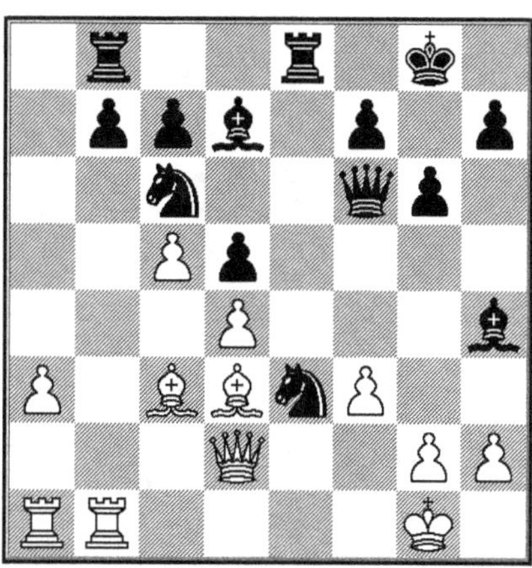

Black has a positional advantage with his outpost Knight. What is the most effective way to demonstrate this?

2 - Smaler Piece Sacrifices

29 - White plays 

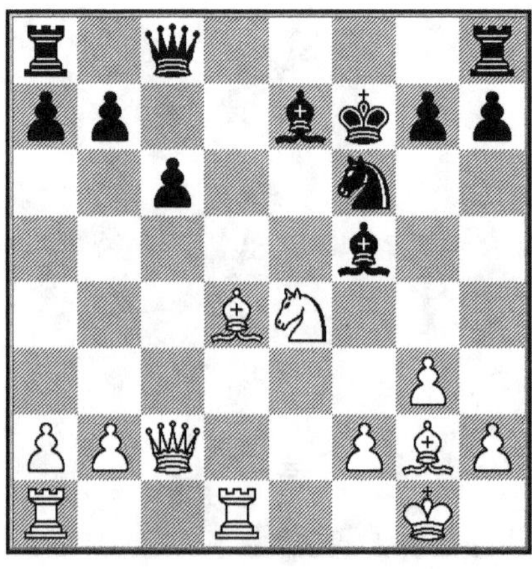

The Black's King is a first-order objective. How would you conduct the attack?

31 - Black plays 

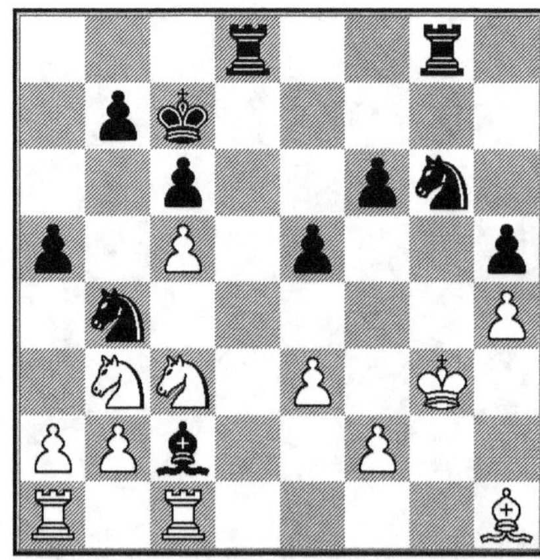

The uncovered are doing very well, but they need to know how to keep going... and win! That's why you're here.

30 - Black plays 

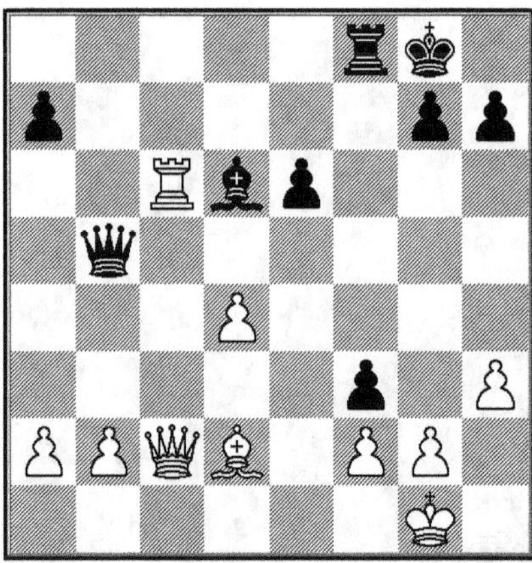

It doesn't look like the stalls are in any imminent danger, but the pawn embedded in f3 bodes ill.

32 - White plays 

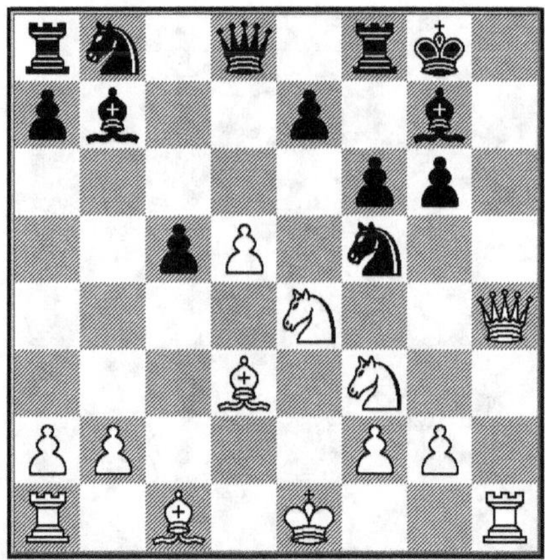

Once again, the h-file is the big clue. But play finely, because the d5-pawn is hanging on.

2 - Smaler Piece Sacrifices

33 - Black plays ★★

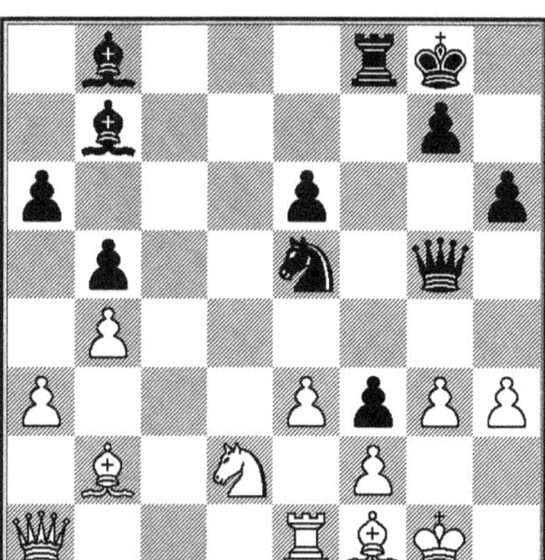

The five Black pieces and the wedge pawn on **f3** are an uncontainable force. It's up to you to release this force.

35 - White plays ★★

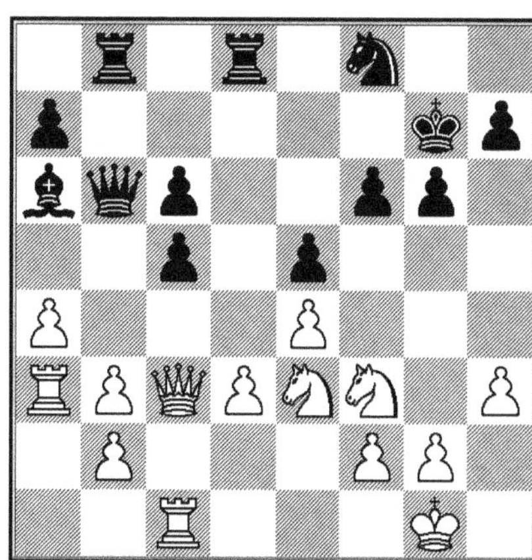

You have to open the can with locksmith technique. With precision and adjustment, taking care of the details.

34 - White plays ★★

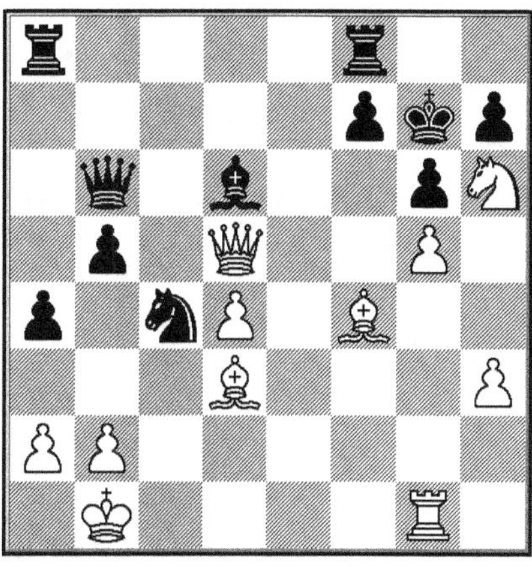

The player with White has played valiantly and will take a 2629 Elo piece here. What should I do?

36 - Black plays ★★

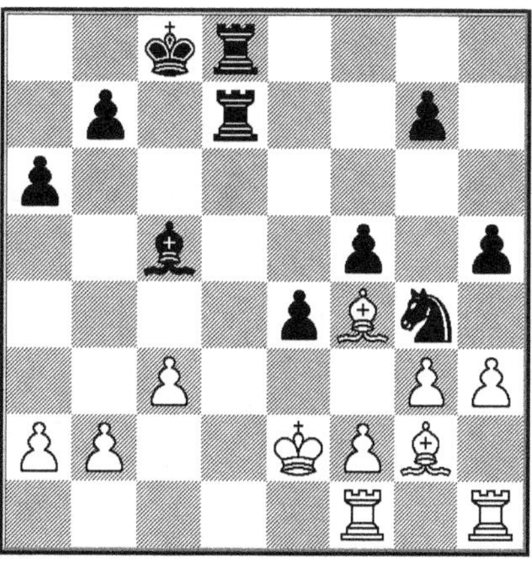

The dominance of the open column and the restrictive effect of the **e4** pawn provide a clear window for Black.

2 - Smaler Piece Sacrifices

37 - White plays 

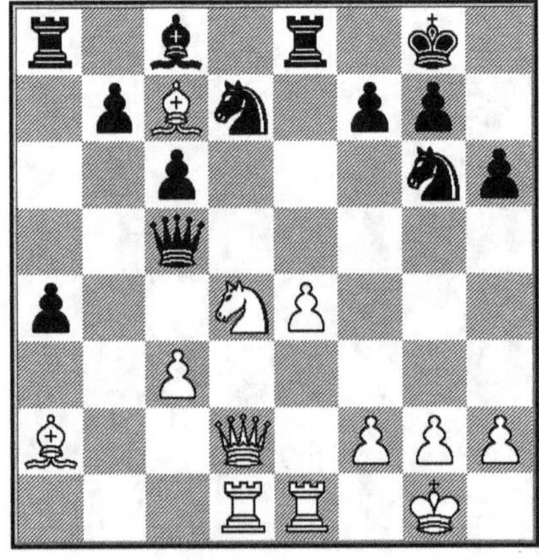

Let's see how a world champion plays. Or better still, how you would play (if you were him) with the white pieces.

39 - White plays 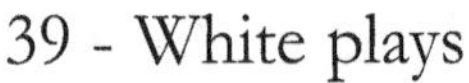

The c4 pawn (passed and advantage) would be a great asset in the endgame, but first you need to know what happens to Black's King.

38 - White plays 

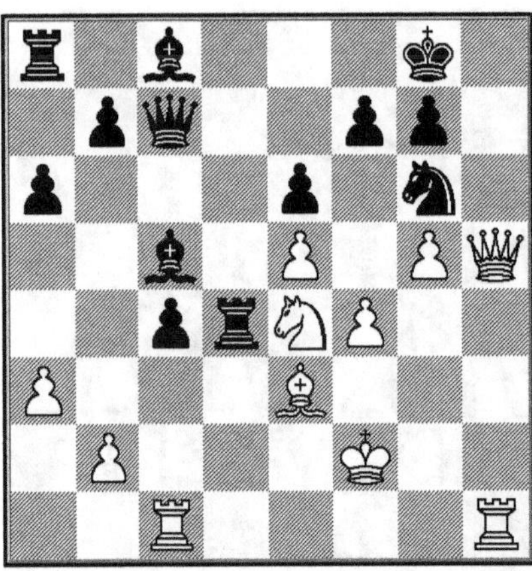

The **h** column won't win on its own and White has already given up a piece. How to continue the attack?

40 - Black plays 

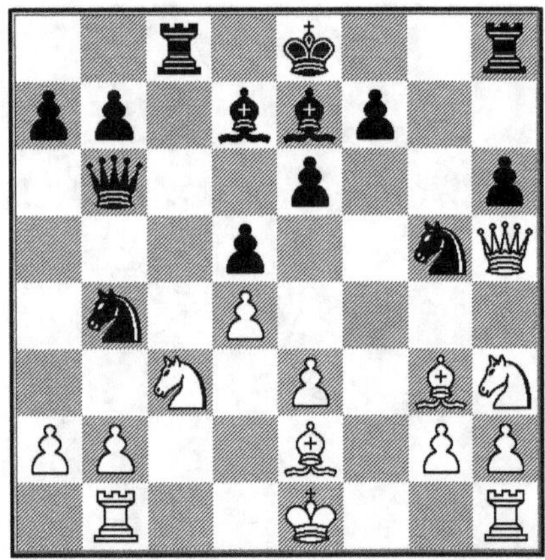

Black pieces are very dynamic and can set up a winning sequence. What will you do?

2 - Smaler Piece Sacrifices

41 - White plays ★★

A very tense situation, but the one that exposes Black's King in the center should tip the scales in White's favour.

43 - White plays ★★

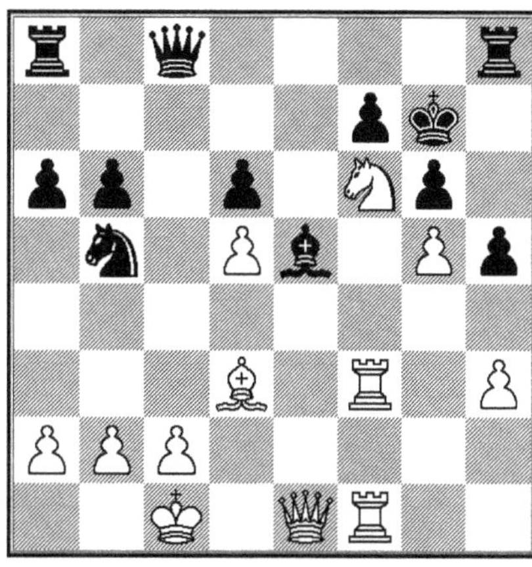

Maximum pressure from the White pieces on the opponent's King, which Satan Beliavsky will convert into a full point.

42 - White plays ★★

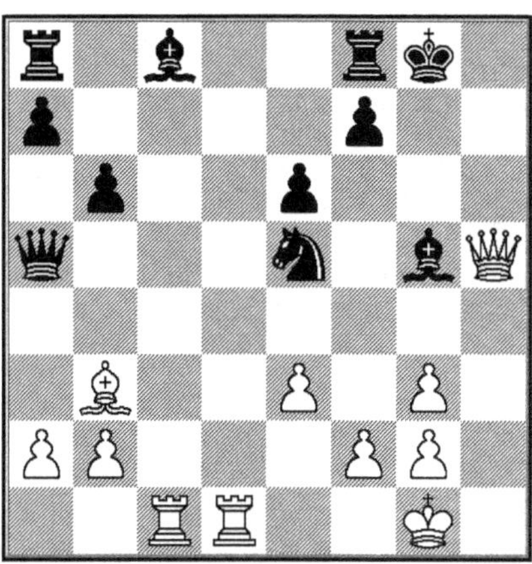

Black has just taken a Knight on g5, but found himself with a surprising answer. Which one?

44 - White plays ★★

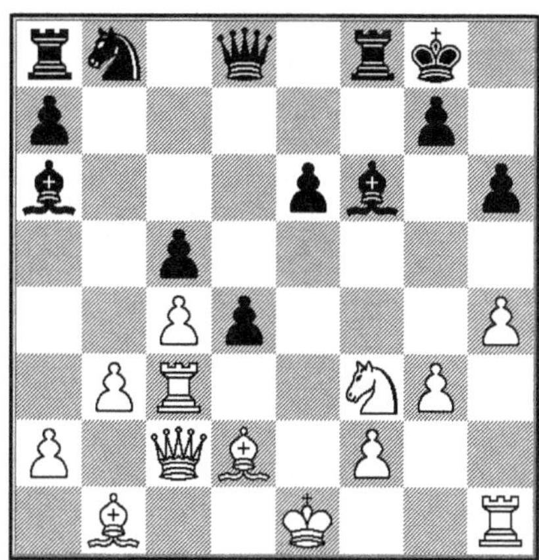

The position is explosive, with White's King in the center and Black's King exposed on the highway to heaven which is the b1–h7 diagonal.

2 - Smaler Piece Sacrifices

45 - White plays ★★★

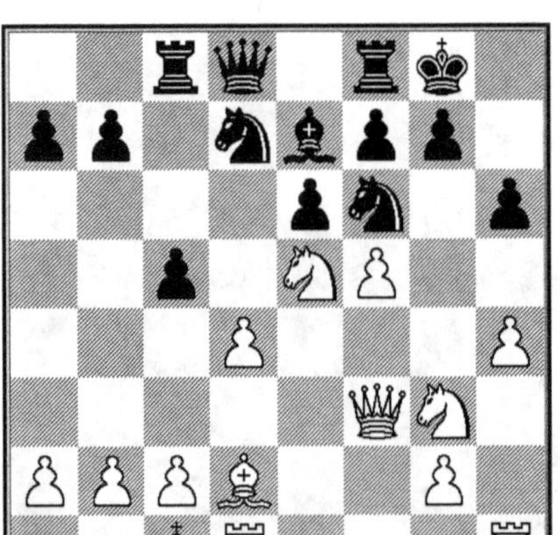

The die is cast. It's a question of calculation and a steady hand. Adjust everything you can...

47 - Black plays ★★★

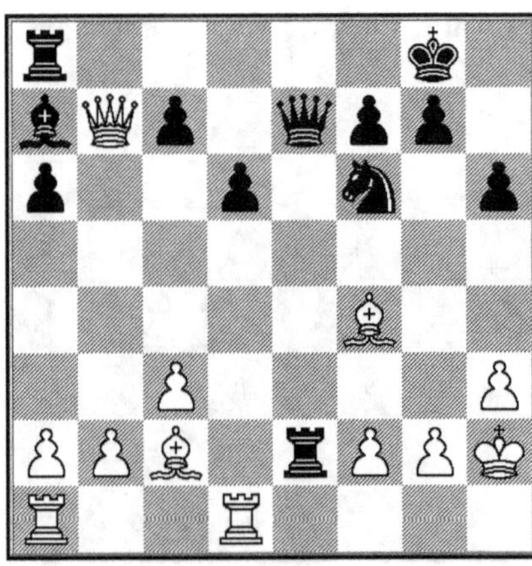

A position that has its tactical intricacies, but certainly held no secrets for the great Ivanchuk.

46 - White plays ★★★

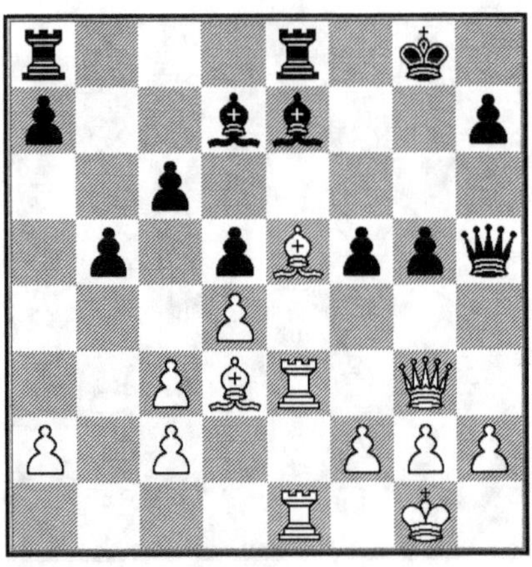

An easy first move and a difficult second. Can you handle the hardest one yet?

48 - White plays ★★★

White faces a dilemma: if 20.♘g6+ ♔f7 21.♗d3 ♔xc3. Dig deeper and solve it.

3 - Various Sacrifices

49 - White plays 

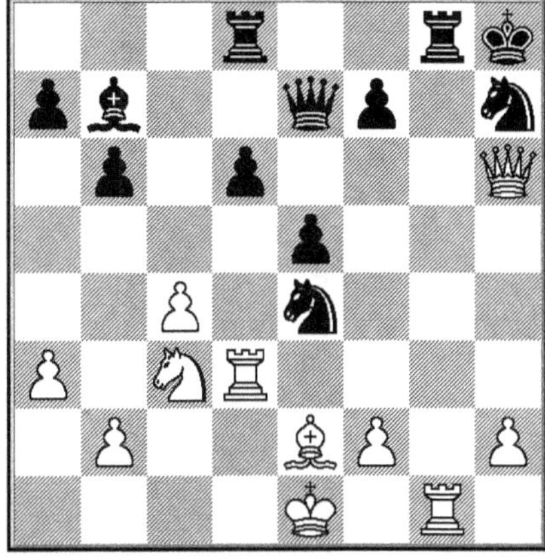

Well, child's play. As soon as... even Magnus Carlsen could solve it!

51 - Black plays 

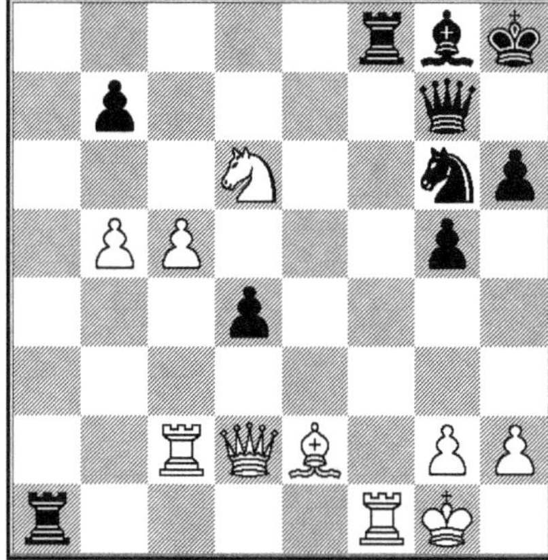

Everything is in place for White's King to be sentenced. The question is how and in what order.

50 - Black plays 

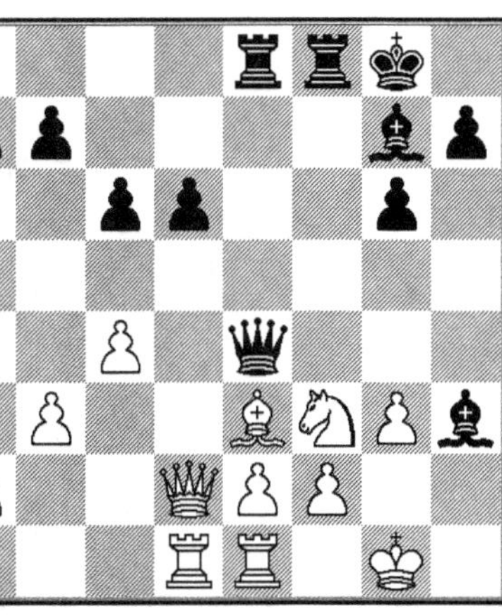

The light squares make water, which is especially significant around the White's King.

52 - White plays 

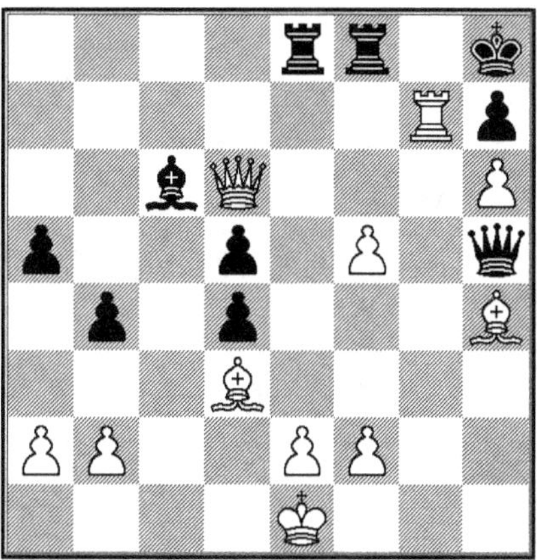

Show us that magic touch that made you famous. How do you win?

3 - Various Sacrifices

53 - White plays ★★

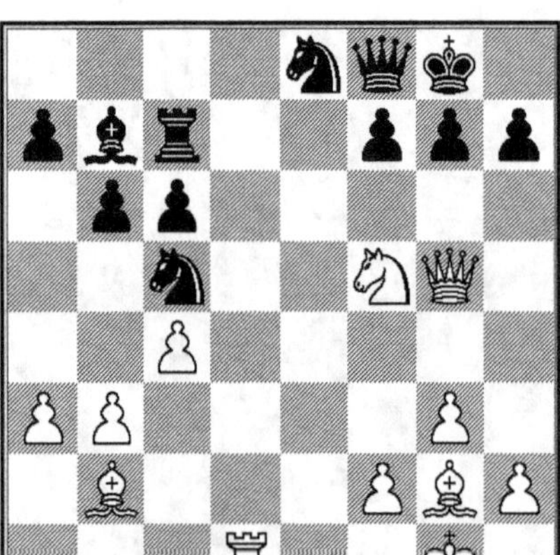

The passivity of the Black pieces contrasts with the great activity of the White pieces. What is the most effective move?

55 - Black plays ★★

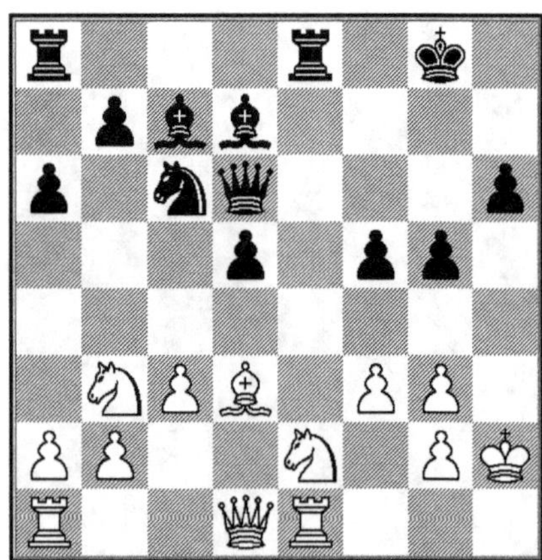

Yes, the first move seems obvious, but can you manage the whole sequence and bring it to a successful conclusion?

54 - Black plays ★★

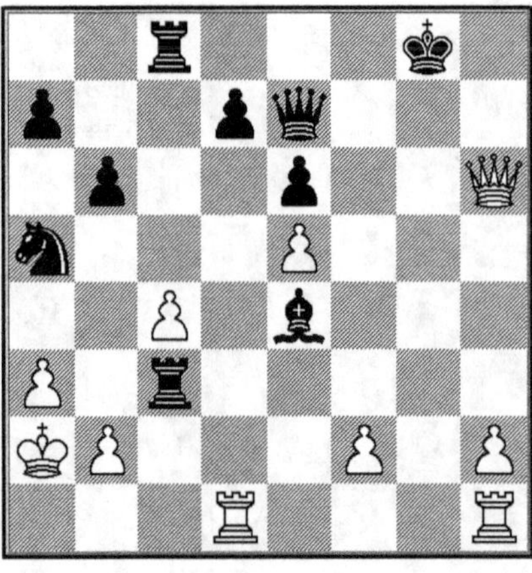

White's threats are fearsome, but it's Black's turn to play!

56 - Black plays ★★

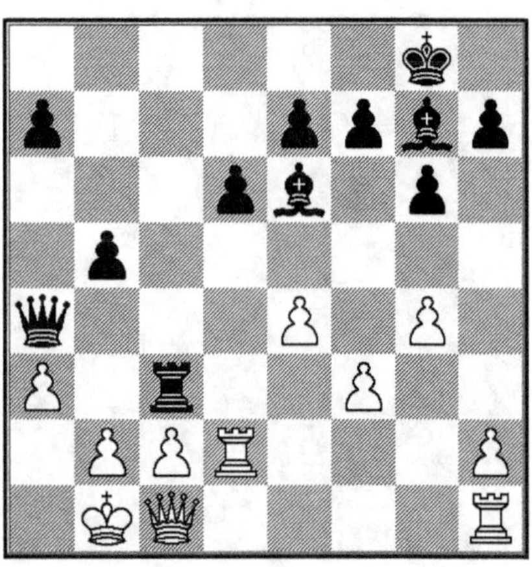

The youngsters look like fierce wolves. Here David Recuero brilliantly finishes off his castling attack.

3 - Various Sacrifices

57 - White plays ★★

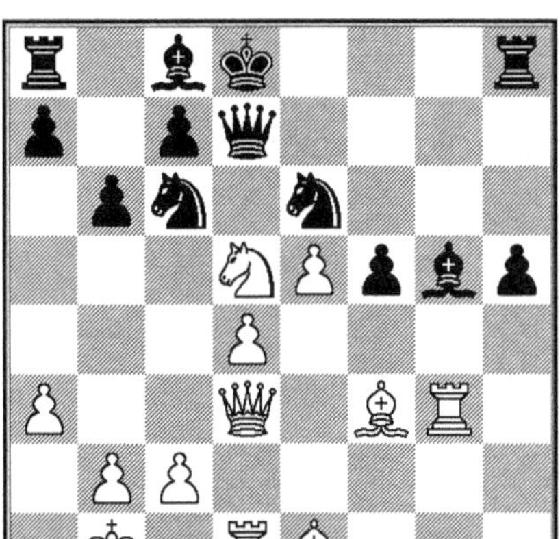

Black have a painful position, due to their King in the center and delayed development. But it needs to be demonstrated!

59 - White plays ★★

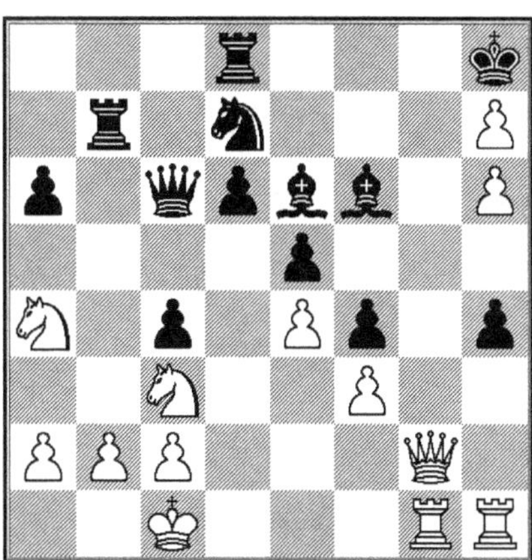

In exchange for a piece, White did a lot of damage to the King's ward. But is there a denouement?

58 - White plays ★★

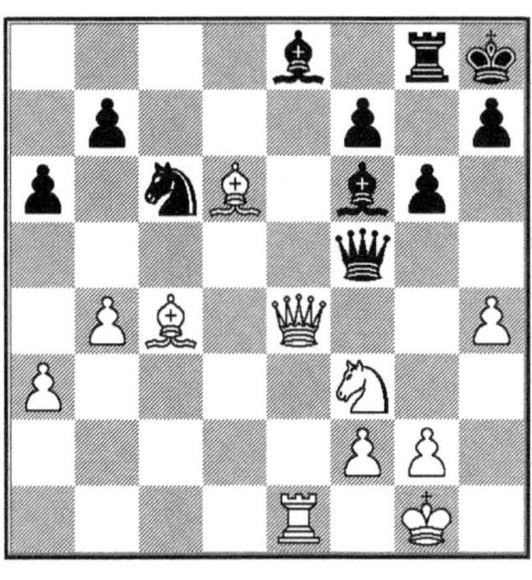

Black made a serious mistake in his last move (**25...♛f5**). Why is it a blunder?

60 - White plays ★★

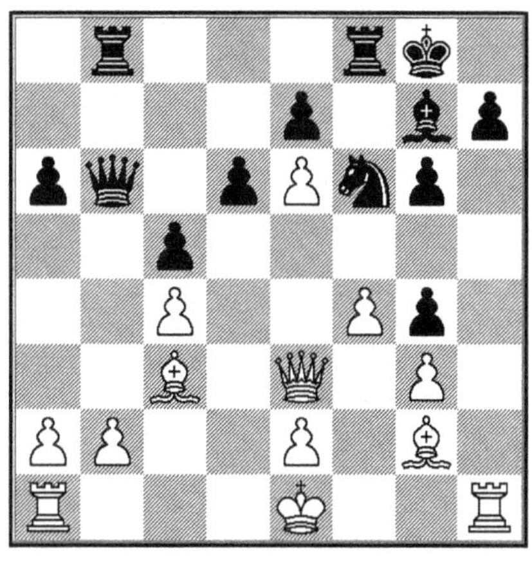

A rather complicated attack, characteristic of Jon Speelman's Laskerian style. Onwards!

3 - Various Sacrifices

61 - White plays ★★

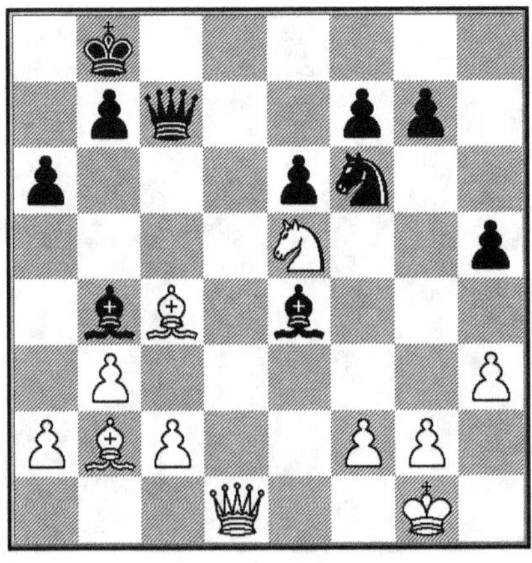

Black's last move, **21...♗e4**, was a mistake. How can we refute it?

62 - White plays ★★

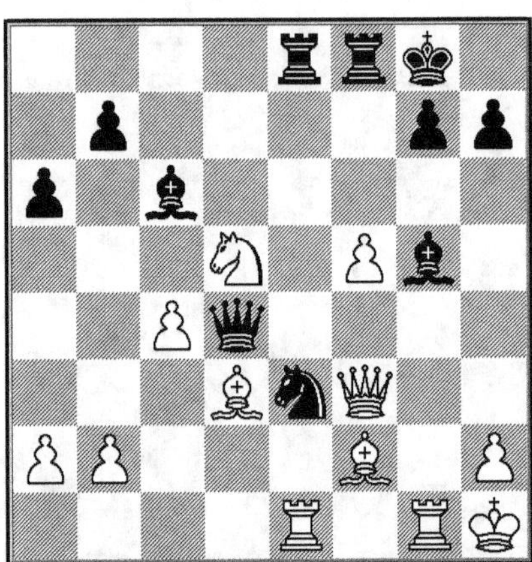

In this confusing position, things will soon become surprisingly clear.

63 - White plays ★★

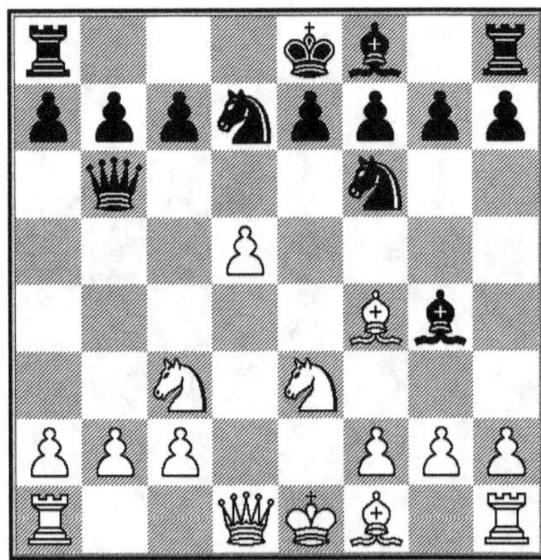

In the case of a double capture on **g4**, Black hoped to recover the piece by taking it on **b2**. But something failed in his calculations. What?

64 - Black plays ★★

If a King is in danger, it's not an endgame. And if it's a middlegame, Bishops of opposite colors favor the attacker.

3 - Various Sacrifices

65 - Black plays ★★

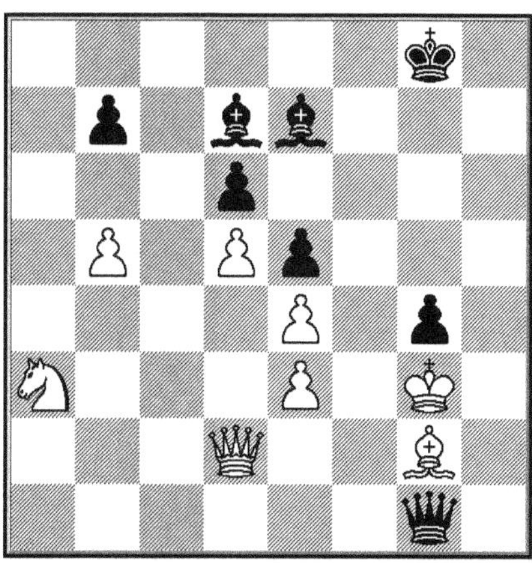

Black pieces are ideally placed to execute a King who only has the protection of his hosts.

67 - White plays ★★

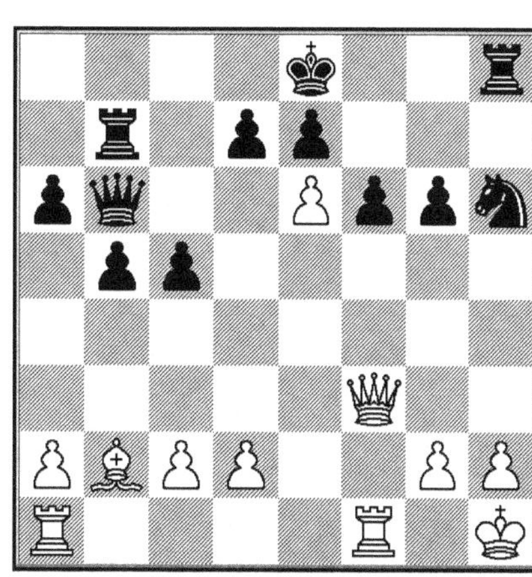

Black's King position is insecure and this compensates for the pawn. But it's not clear how White should continue.

66 - White plays ★★

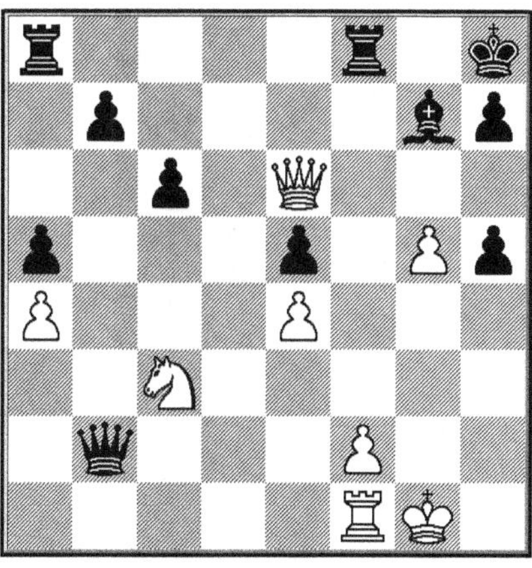

The intrepid Judit Polgár performs one of her fearsome combinations here. How does she do it?

68 - White plays ★★

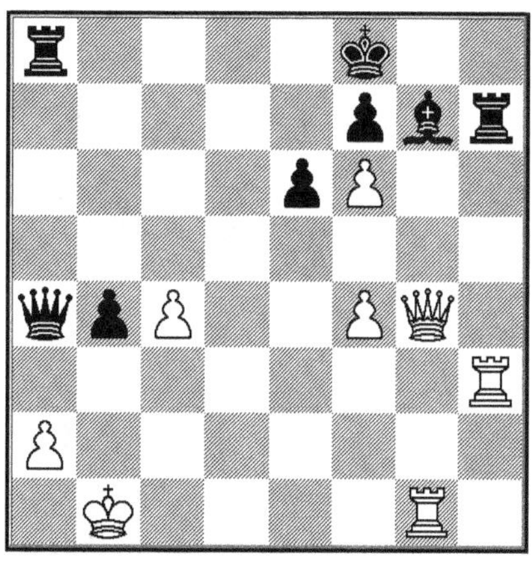

Both Kings are exposed, but White has a decisive card right away. It's all about playing it.

3 - Various Sacrifices

69 - White plays ★★

All the work is done. All that's left is to finish it off, but... nothing less!

71 - Black plays ★★

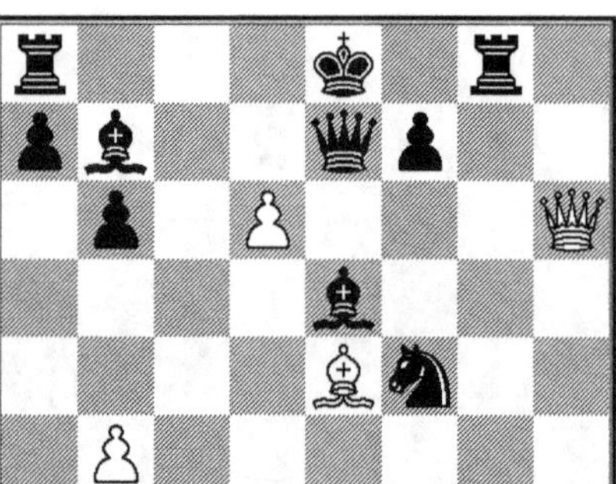

The combination has all the more merit when it takes place in an under-14 World Championship.

70 - White plays ★★

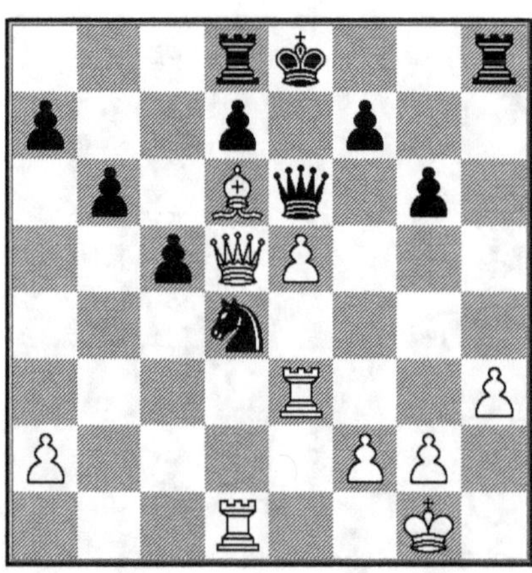

Artur Yusupov's elegant precision is evident in this beautiful combinatorial sequence.

72 - White plays ★★

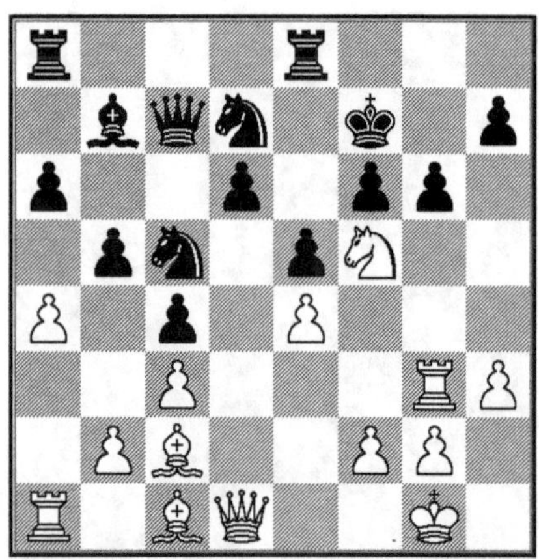

Black's position seems flexible and resilient, but there is a certain weakness around his King. How would you play?

3 - Various Sacrifices

73 - Black plays ★★

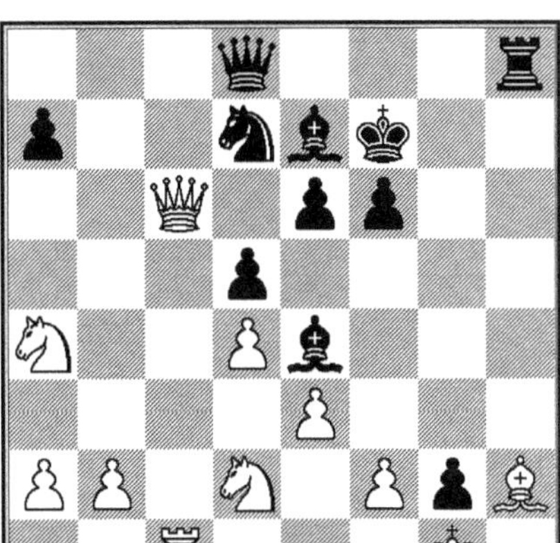

The King of Whites is in danger, as Cuban GM Julio Becerra will demonstrate.

75 - White plays ★★

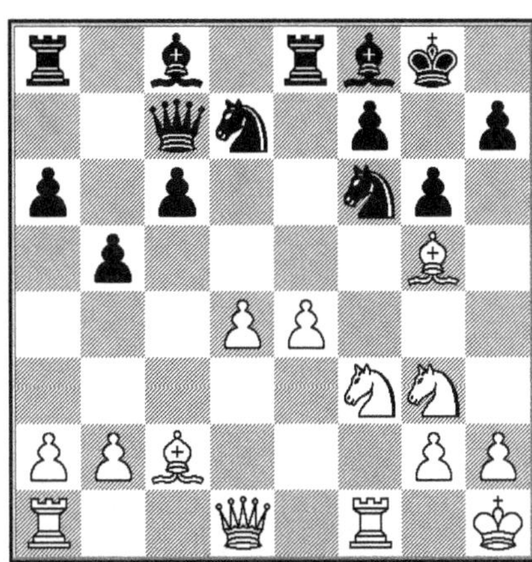

With his last move, **15...g6**, Black aggravated some problems in his position, such as the weakness of f7.

74 - White plays ★★

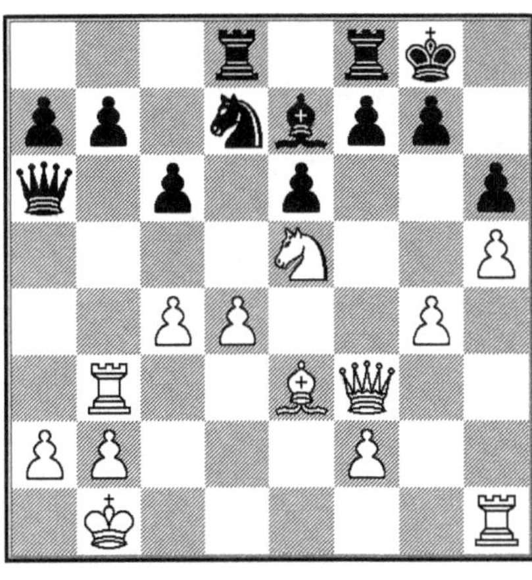

How can the Black's King be reached? Seek the subtlety of the master.

76 - Black plays ★★

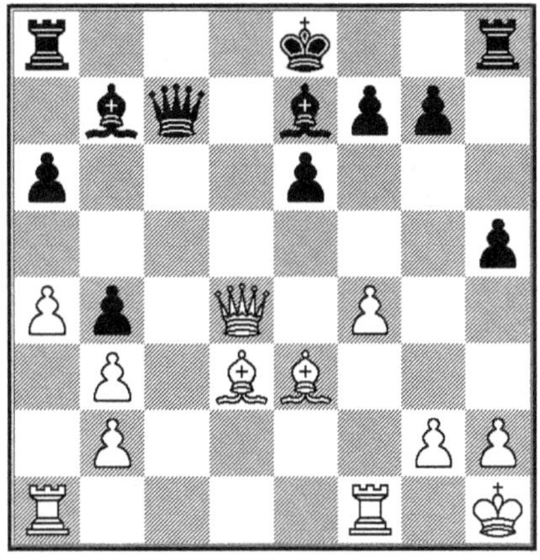

The normal here would be ...♕d8, entering a good ending, but Pia Cramling finds a very original tactical plan.

3 - Various Sacrifices

77 - White plays ★★★

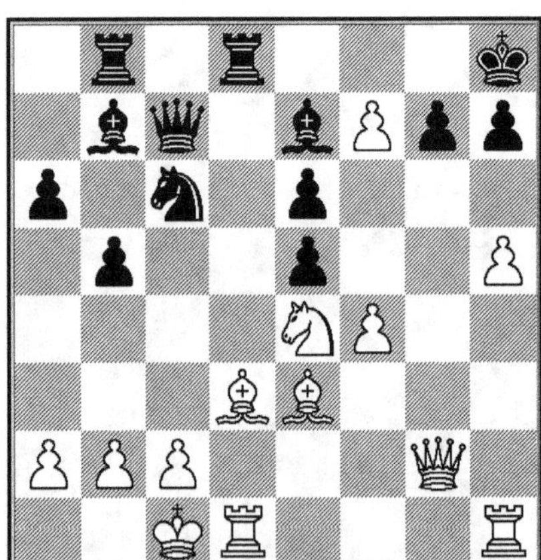

The Black's King situation really is precarious and he should be afraid of the relentless blows you will deliver.

79 - White plays ★★★

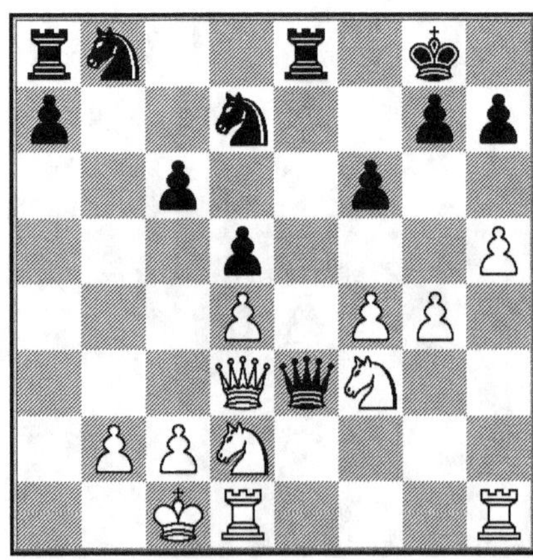

Humpy Koneru, the extraordinary Indian player, has just played **22...♛e3**. Why is it a mistake? (it's not easy).

78 - White plays ★★★

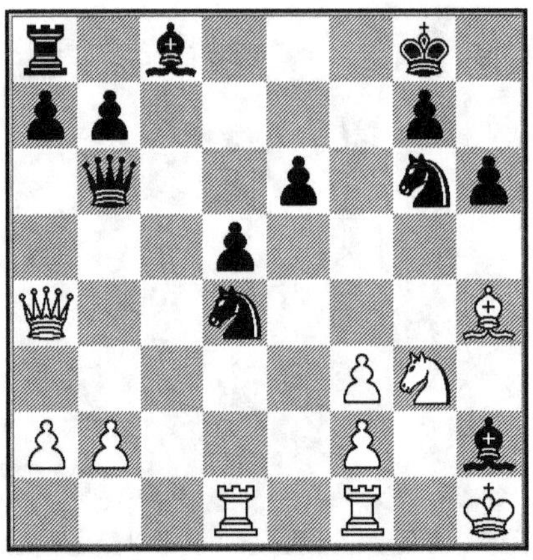

In this tricky position Black has just taken a bishop on **g6**. What's the optimal sequence for White?

80 - White plays ★★★

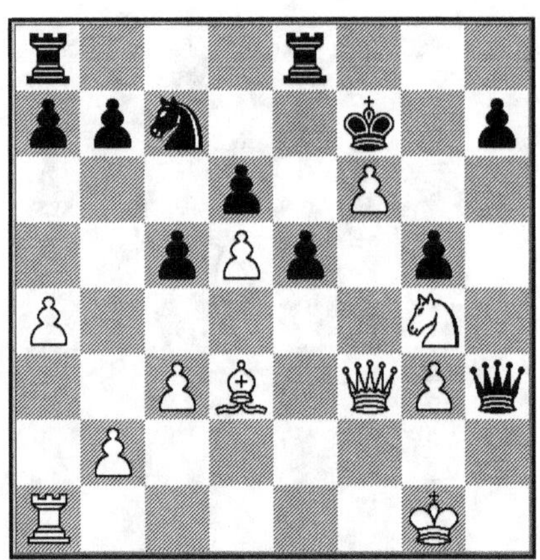

Black has an advantage, but an exposed King. On the other hand, what happens to the Black Queen?

4 - Queen and Multiple Sacrifices

81 - White plays 

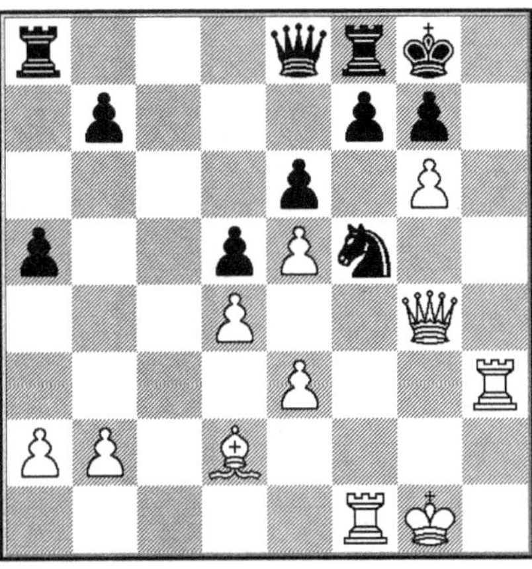

A sung combination, if you know the basic themes.

83 - White plays 

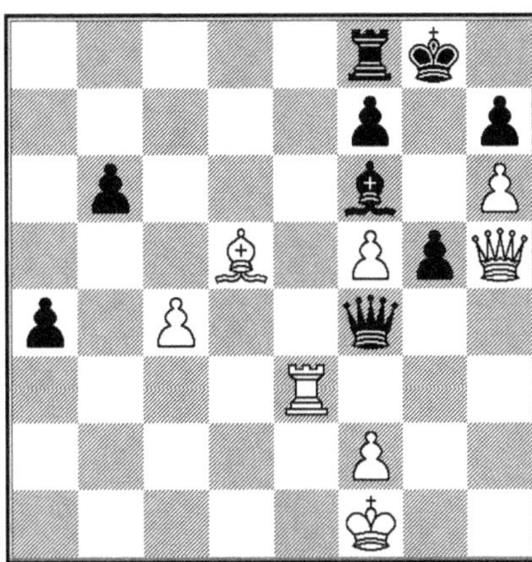

Probably in a time crunch, Black made an unforgivable mistake with **37...a4?** How to punish?

82 - White plays 

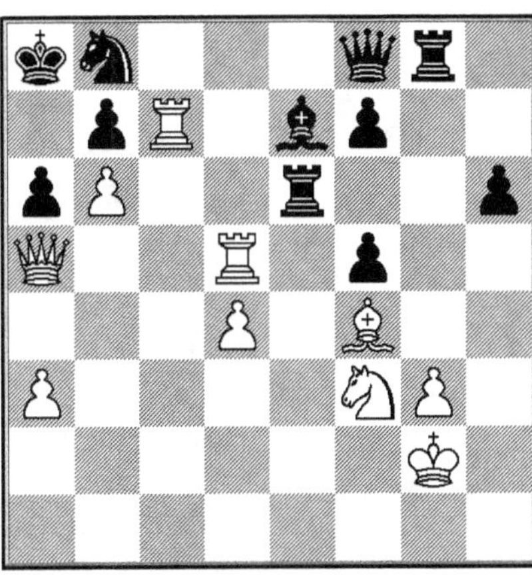

White have achieved a very dominant position and are ready to strike the definitive blow. How?

84 - White plays 

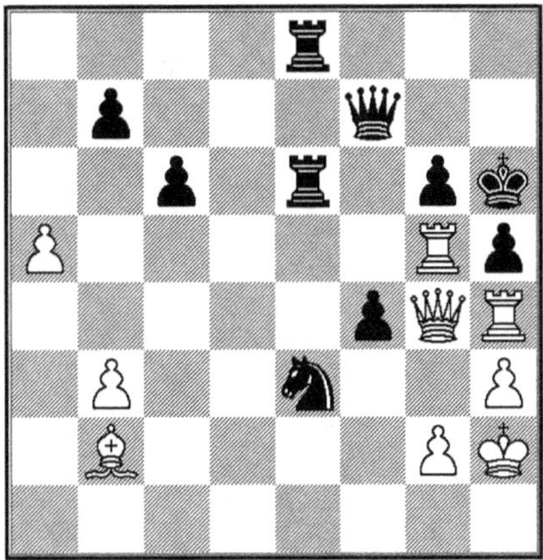

A small puzzle. Nothing you can't solve in the blink of an eye.

4 - Queen and Multiple Sacrifices

85 - Black plays ★★

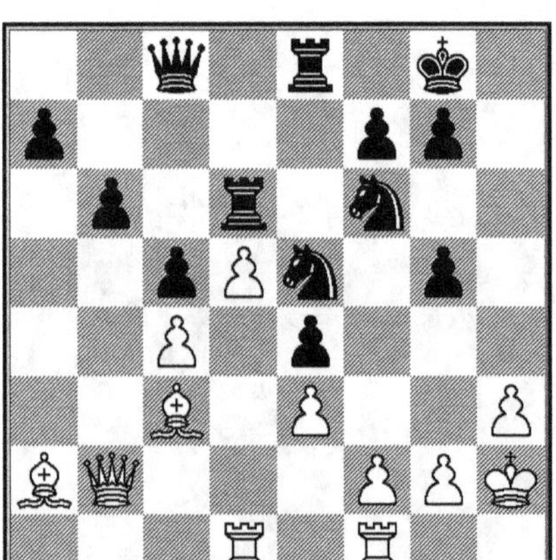

White's King has run out of defenders, and the black pieces are ready for the final invasion.

87 - Black plays ★★

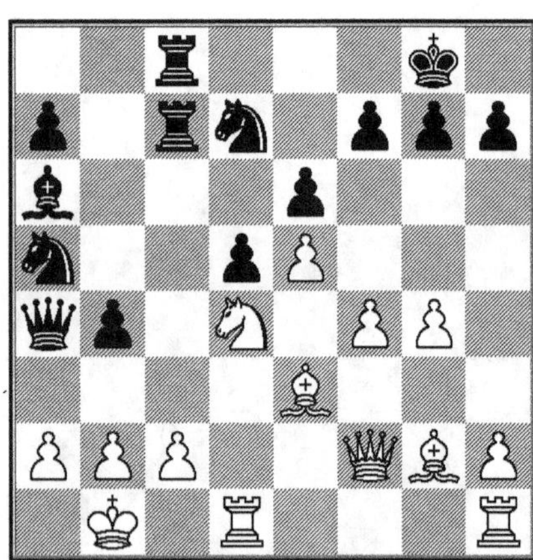

Black has moved ahead in the attacking race and has a decisive sequence. Which one?

86 - Black plays ★★

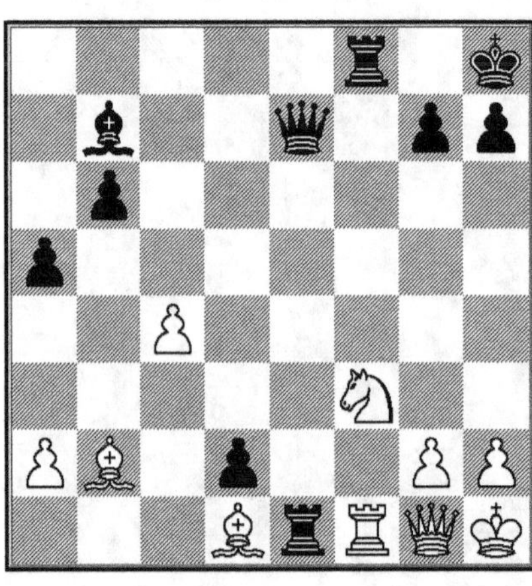

A 2598 Elo at the age of 15 is not within everyone's reach. Fabiano Caruana is another of today's young phenoms.

88 - White plays ★★

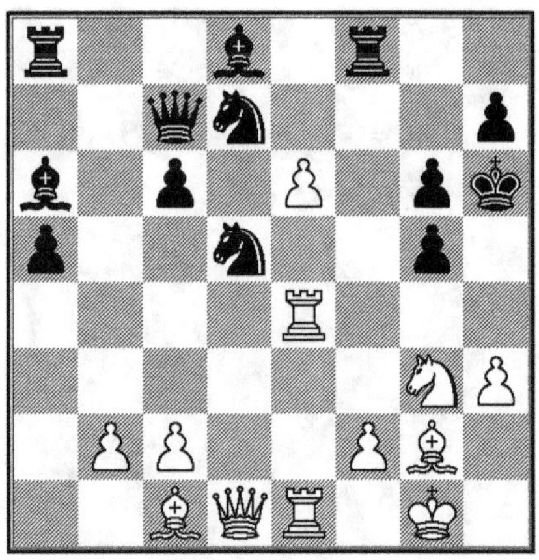

White sacrificed a piece for the attack. Can you think of any coherent continuation?

4 - Queen and Multiple Sacrifices

89 - White plays 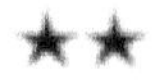

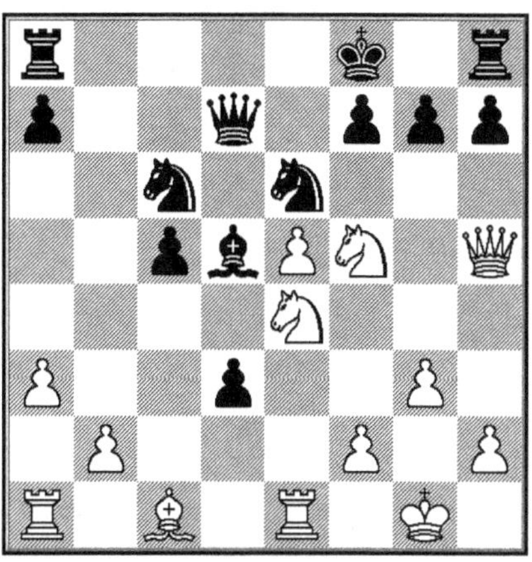

The arrangement of the White pieces is very threatening, as if to make it look like there is something there, and you are the one who has to find it.

91 - Black plays 

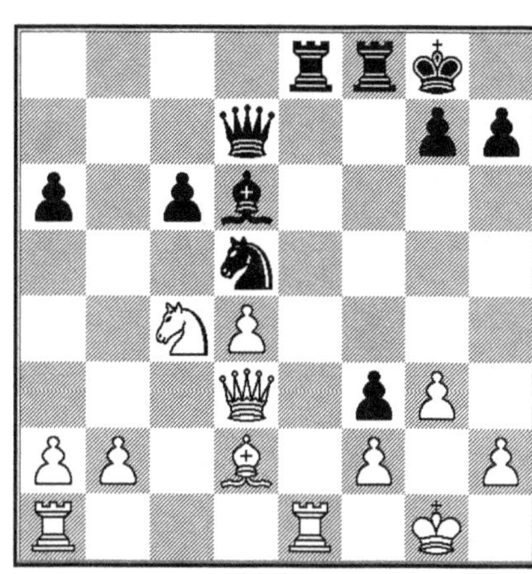

In this Marshall Attack, Black's pawn embedded on f3 bodes ill for White, who is enveloped in brilliance.

90 - Black plays 

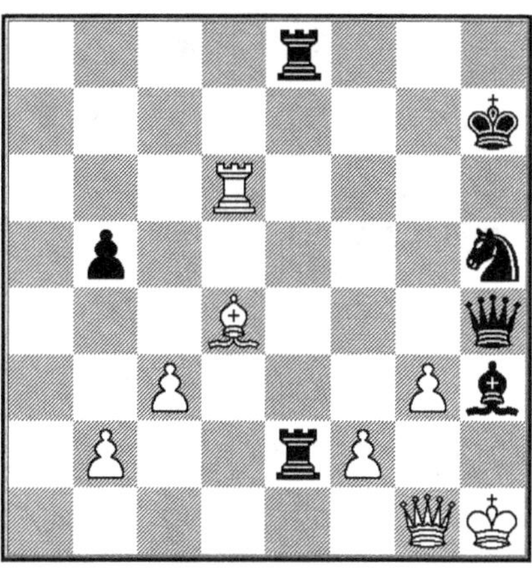

White has four pawns for the piece, but his King needs urgent attention. What would you play?

92 - White plays 

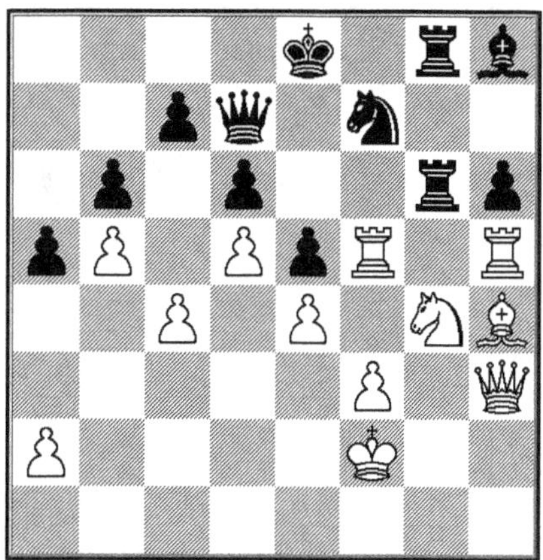

White has more space and dominant pieces, but it's not easy to see how to penetrate the enemy camp.

4 - Queen and Multiple Sacrifices

93 - Black plays ★★★

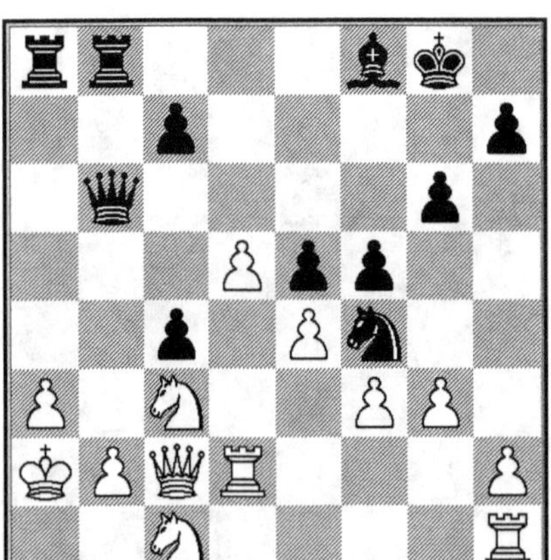

An atypical position, derived from a Sämisch Attack, in which Black considers that the time has come to act.

95 - White plays ★★★

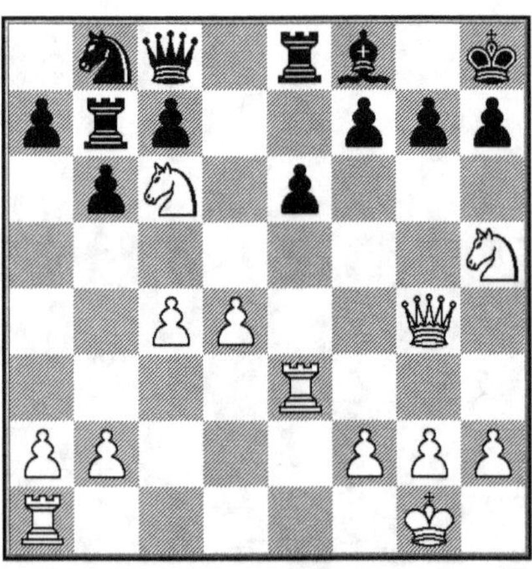

Whites have a considerable advantage due to their greater space and better coordination of troops.

94 - White plays ★★★

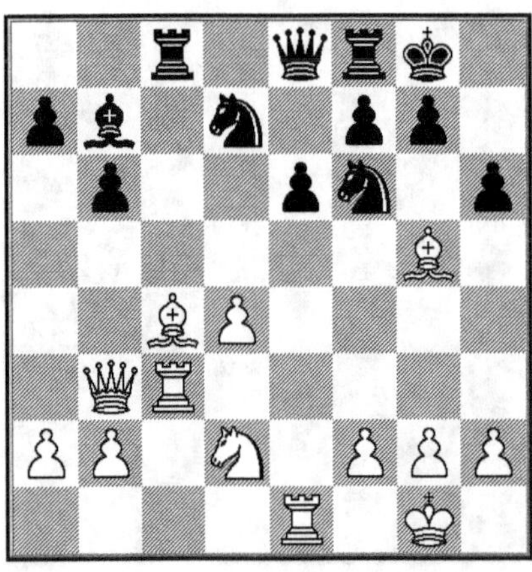

White pieces (with a Rook already on the third row) are perfectly placed to respond to the provocation.

96 - White plays ★★★

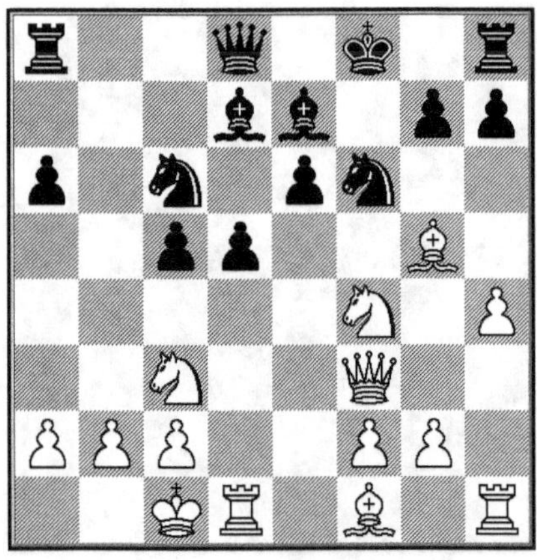

Great positioning of the White pieces, to which the Black ones seem to oppose a solid position. How do you see it?

4 - Queen and Multiple Sacrifices

97 - White plays ★★★

White has a winning position due to the excellent arrangement of pieces and the magnificent **b1–h7** diagonal. Ideal?

99 - White plays ★★★

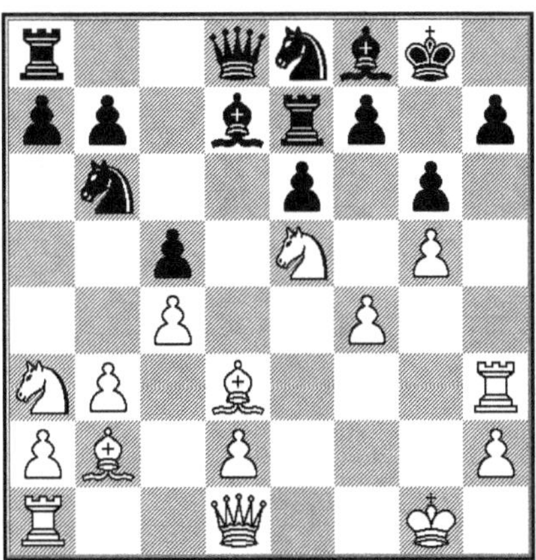

Tomas Oral, a positional player of the highest calibre, applies a combinatorial lesson to his compatriot David Navara.

98 - Black plays ★★★

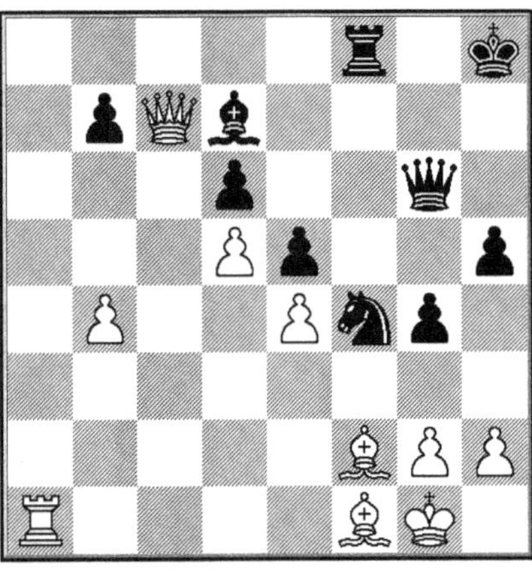

Don't dive into the solution that seems so clear, because you'll have to figure out a few small details first.

100 - White plays ★★★

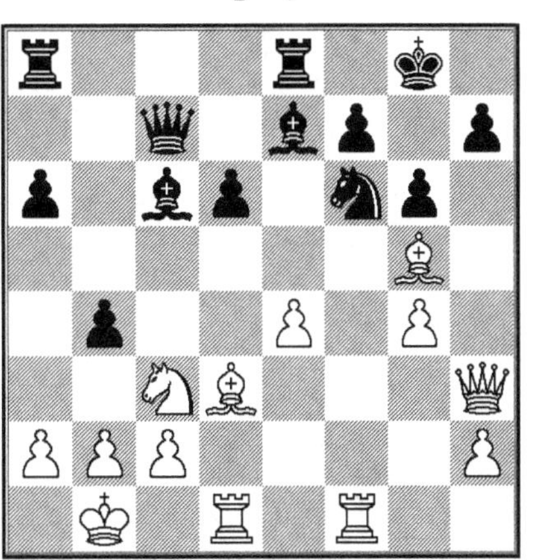

Both pieces attacked... Which is more decisive? Without a doubt, the turn to play.

4 - Queen and Multiple Sacrifices

101 - White plays  ★★★

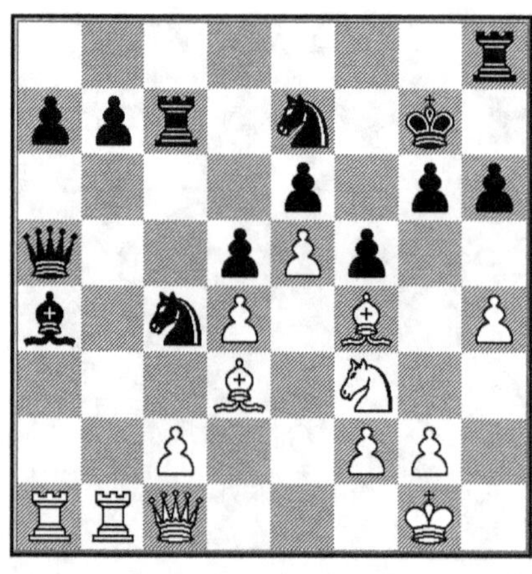

Black says he will resist and has taken the a-pawn. Do you see any way of neutralizing it?

103 - White plays  ★★★

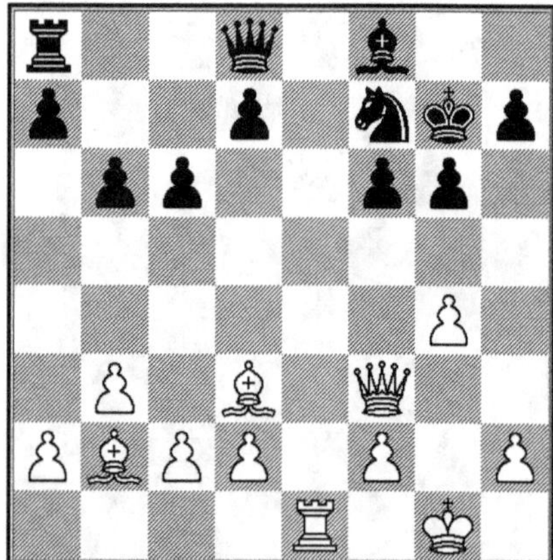

The great difference in the quality of the pieces, together with the pronounced weakness of the f6 square, portend a quick outcome.

102 - Black plays  ★★★

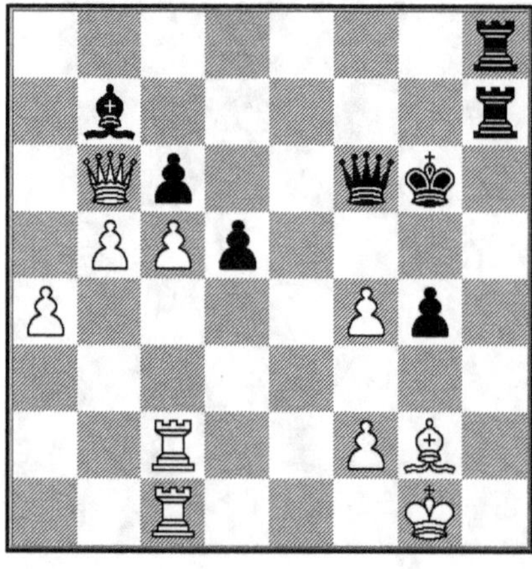

In this fight between heavyweights, there are two dominant factors: the h column and the white pawns of the Queen's wing.

104 - Black plays  ★★★

The pressure of the Black Rooks and the dominance of the large diagonal a8–h1 bode ill for White.

4 - Queen and Multiple Sacrifices

105 - Black plays ★★★

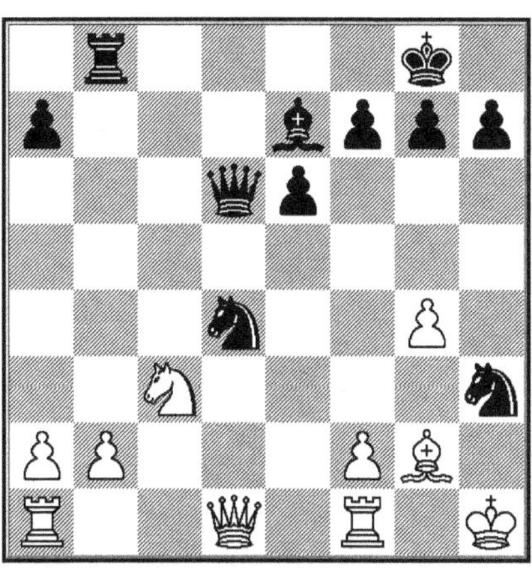

Black sacrificed material to expose White's King. How would you proceed?

107 - Black plays ★★★

Black has undoubtedly won the strategic game and is about to strike the tactical blow. What do you suggest?

106 - Black plays ★★★

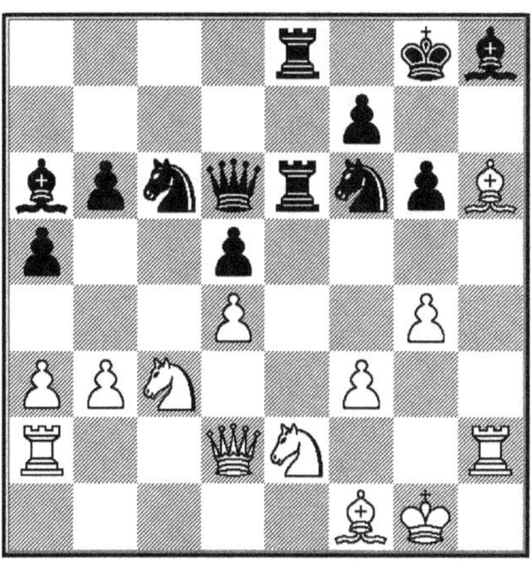

White's weakened castling, dominance of the open spine and latent threats on d4 and e1. How to exploit these factors?

108 - White plays ★★★

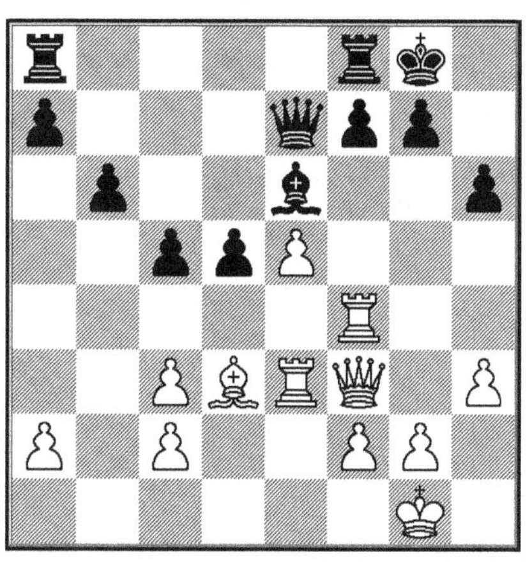

It seems that the ...c4 threat conditions White's attack, but the latter takes aggressive action.

4 - Queen and Multiple Sacrifices

109 - Black plays 

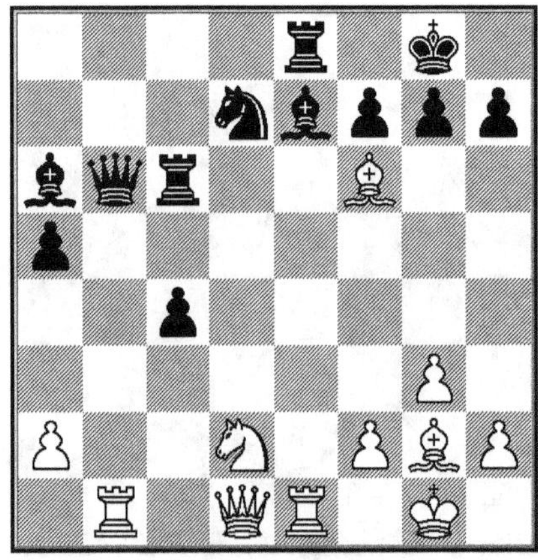

White has just played **25.♗×f6** and falls victim to a superb combination, which you will discover.

111 - White plays 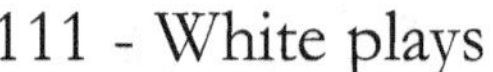

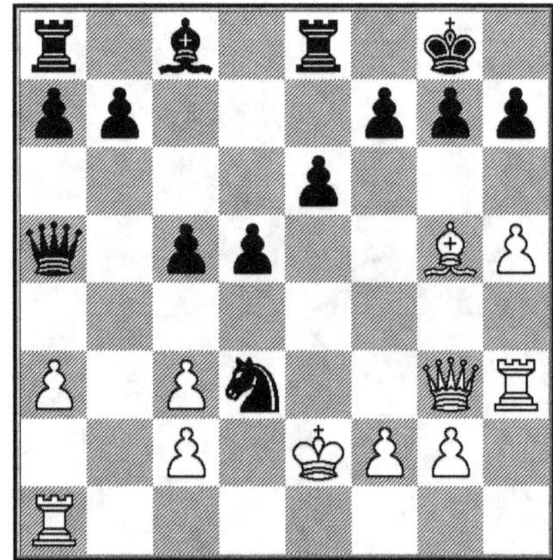

Black, two pawns ahead, has just taken a bishop on **d3**. How would you proceed?

110 - White plays 

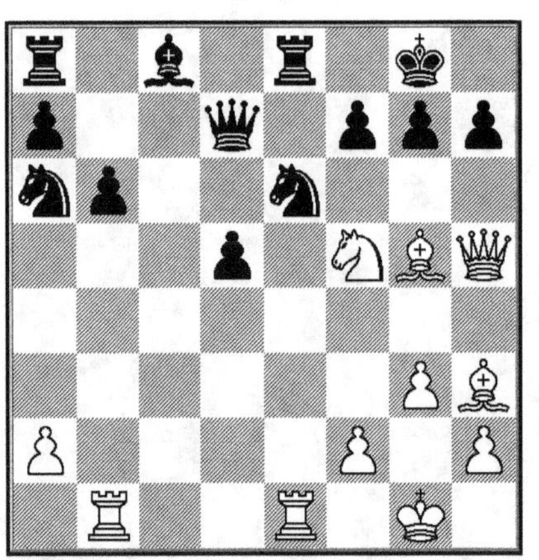

Black has two pawns, but it's doubtful that he'll be able to organise the defence without completing the development.

112 - White plays 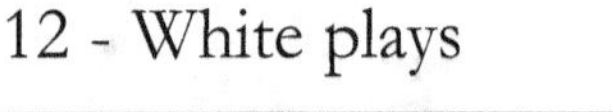

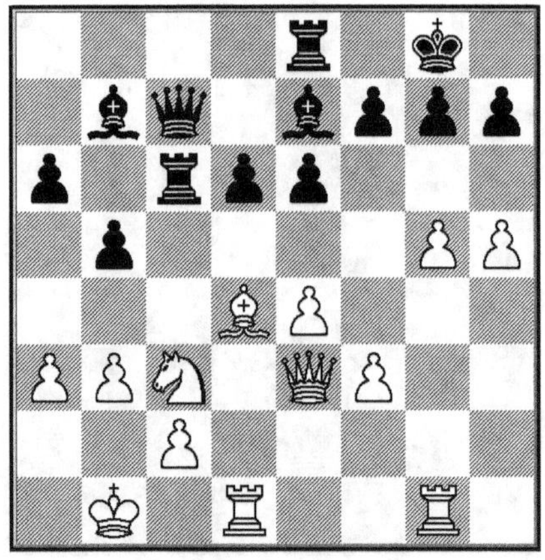

If we had any doubts about Ivanchuk's category, this brilliant blindfolded game would clear things up.

4 - Queen and Multiple Sacrifices

113 - Black plays ★★★

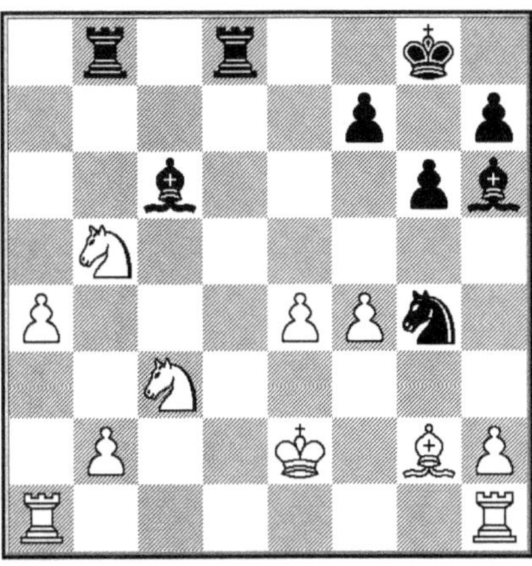

White isn't worried about the f4 pawn, because if 25...♗×f4, 26.♔f3. How should Black proceed?

115 - White plays ★★★

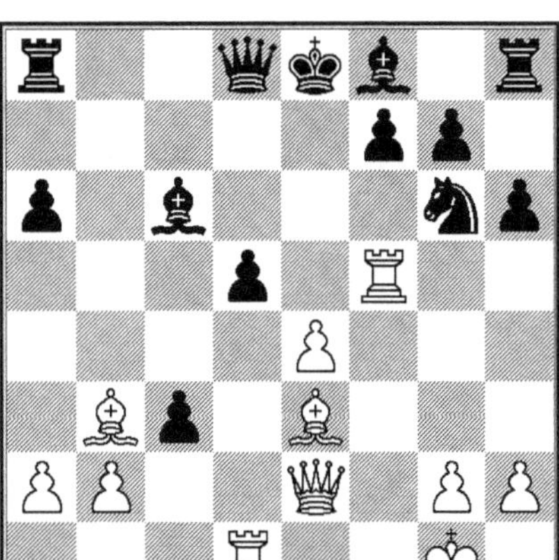

White have sacrificed a piece and the fight is at its critical moment. What do you propose?

114 - White plays ★★★

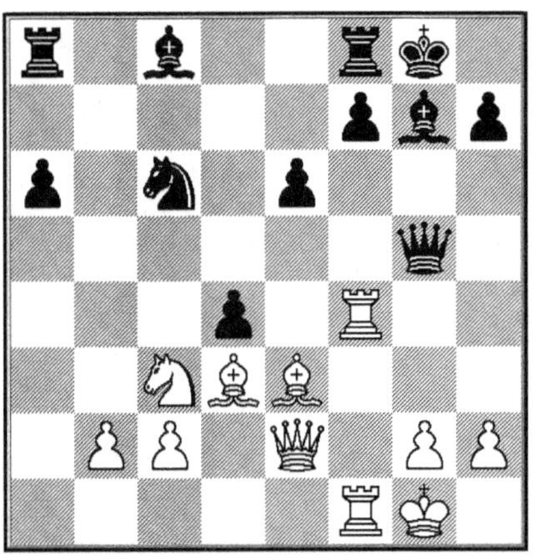

In spite of such a notorious underdevelopment, Black are scratching with their Queen. Something that Short cannot leave unpunished.

116 - Black plays ★★★

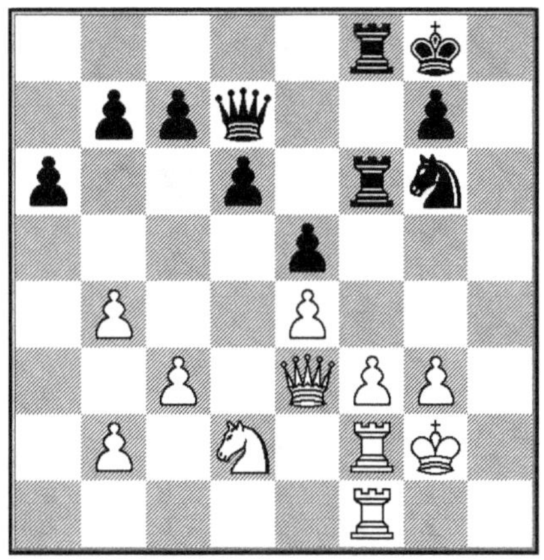

Black, with his four magnificently coordinated pieces, exerts a very strong latent pressure on White's castling.

4 - Queen and Multiple Sacrifices

117 - White plays ★★★

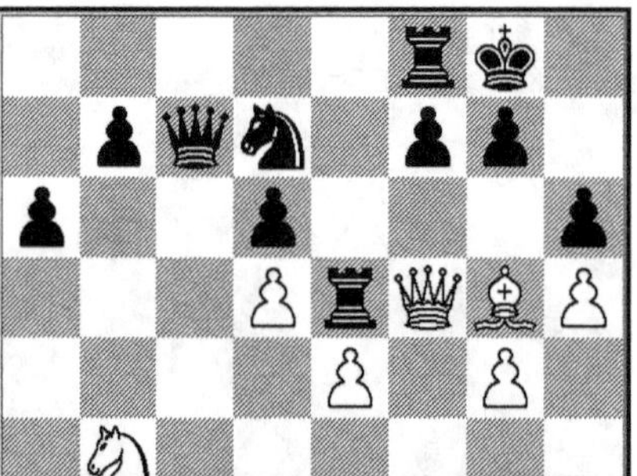

The magician Motylev pulls an incredible piece out of his hat. Seen and unseen! What do you see?

119 - Black plays ★★★

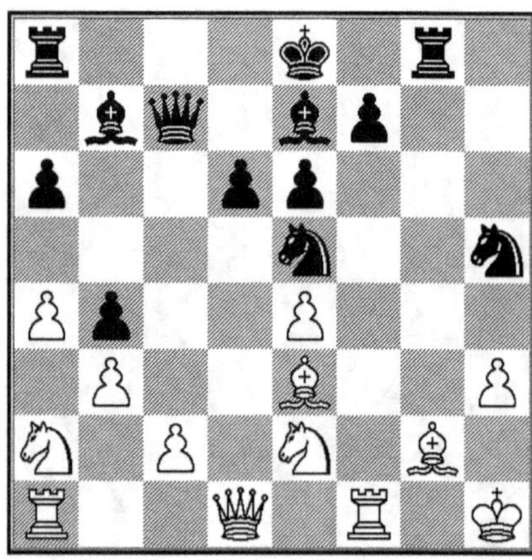

Although the White pieces seem well arranged, the disappearance of the f and g pawns creates uncertainty around the King.

118 - White plays ★★★

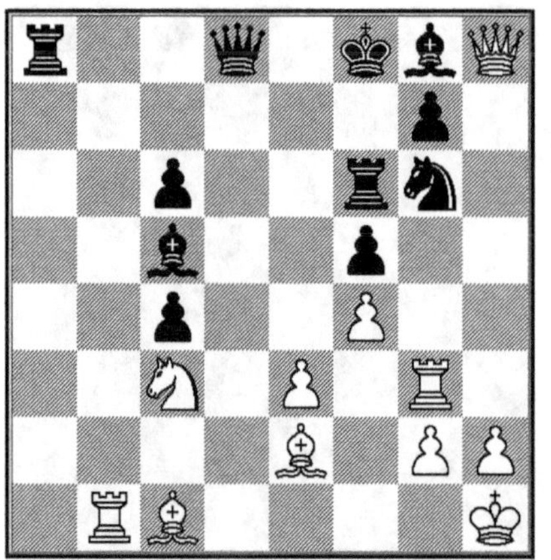

A great combination from one of the greats that you'll have the opportunity to emulate.

120 - White plays ★★★

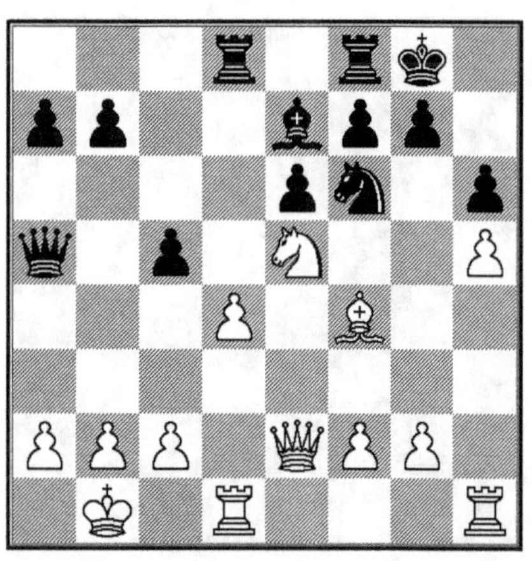

Black's position looks solid, but young Carlsen will take care of dismantling it with a fireworks display.

4 - Queen and Multiple Sacrifices

121 - White plays ★★★

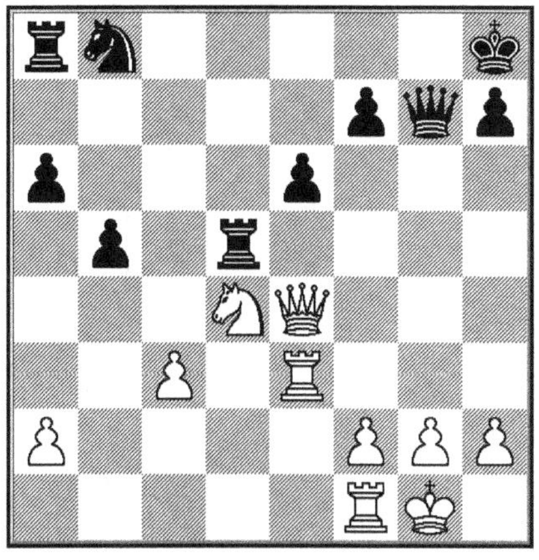

Black's underdevelopment here allows for a speculative combination, in which all the pieces end up fitting together.

123 - White plays ★★★

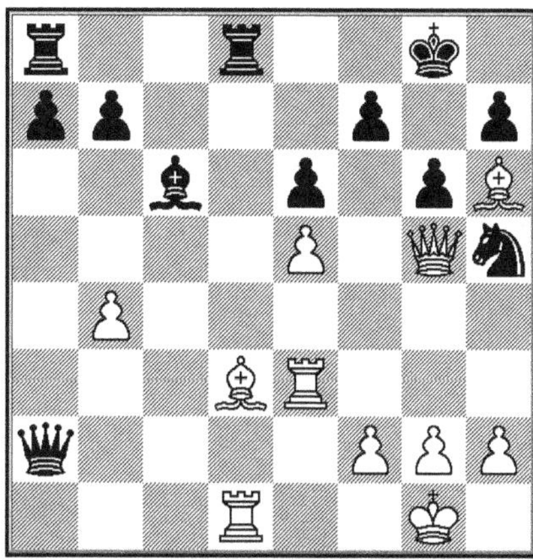

It's about tickling the Black, whose castling is weakened in the squares of their color. But how?

122 - White plays ★★★

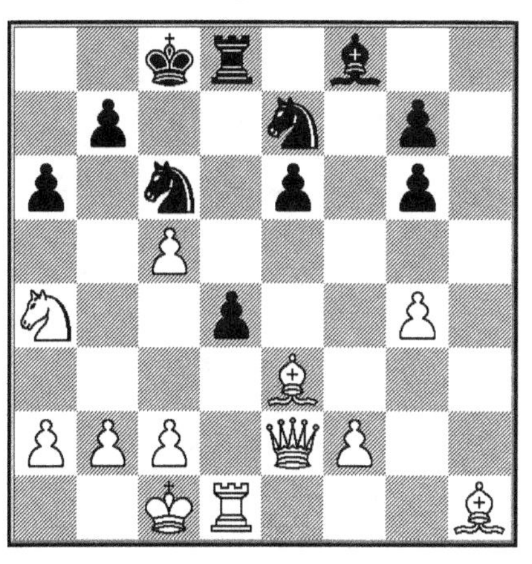

Nicolas Giffard, a two-time French champion, is struggling to cope with the momentum of the new generation. What do you suggest?

124 - Black plays ★★★

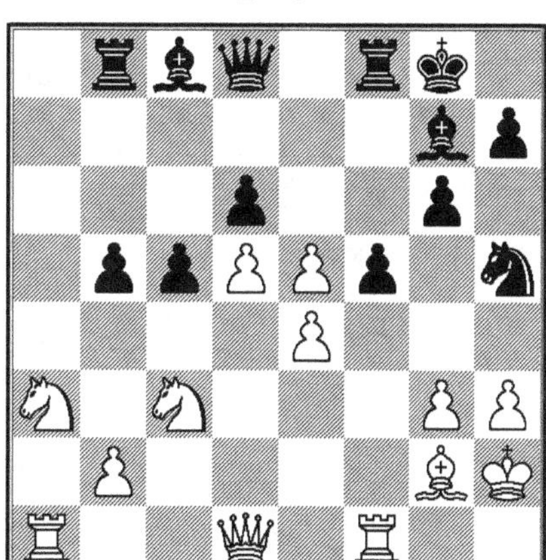

With their last move, **19.f×e5**, White allows a discomfort on b4. But the key is not on the Queen's wing.

4 - Queen and Multiple Sacrifices

125 - White plays  ★★★

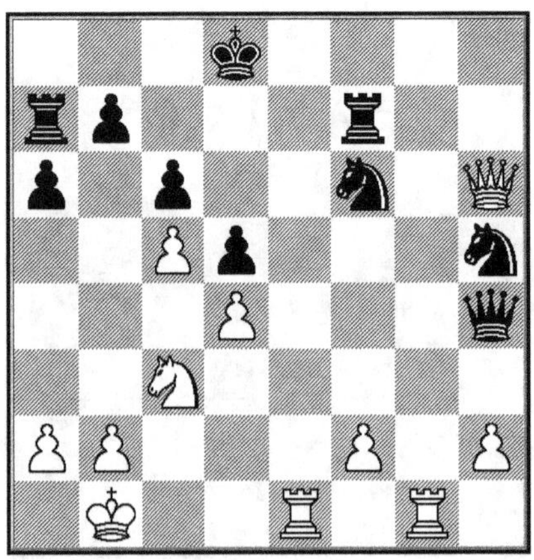

White sacrificed a piece to put his opponent's King on the move. The question now is how to continue the attack.

127 - White plays  ★★★

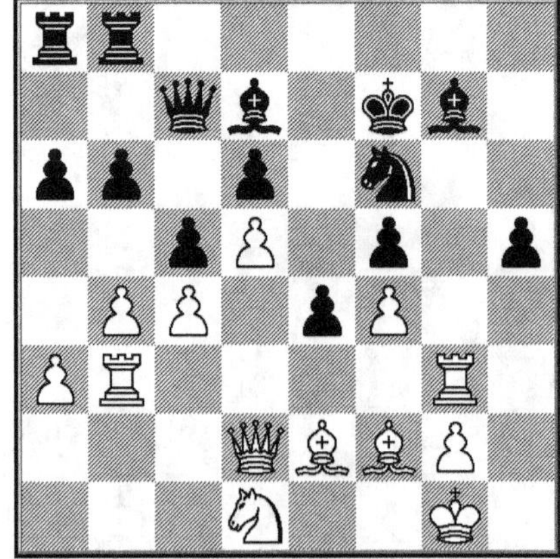

Black's Kingside is a sieve and this, together with the flexibility of the white pieces, makes you fear for your safety.

126 - White plays  ★★★

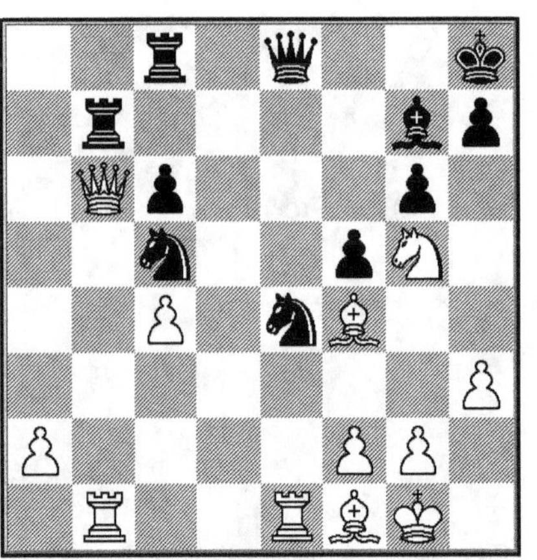

It's not bad to see two world champions in a quick game. White speculates with his more dynamic pieces.

128 - White plays  ★★★

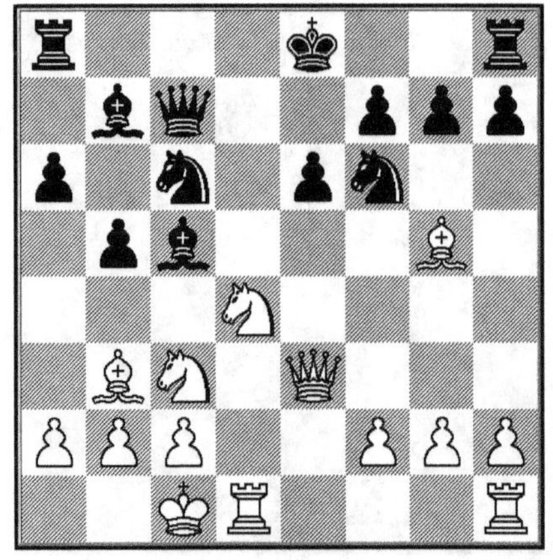

High-voltage game, not recommended for heart patients. There are no clues: you're alone in the middle of the jungle.

SOLUTIONS

1 - ROOK SACRIFICES

1. 29...R×h2+! (0–1). 30.K×h2 Qh4++. Karpov-Shirov, Bastia (rapid), 2.11.2003.

2. 29...R×a3+! (0–1). 30.b×a3 Qb1++; 30.K×a3 Qa1++. Arlandi-Kveinis, Calviá Olympiad, 25.10.2004.

3. 28.R×g6+! h×g6 29.Qh8+ (1–0). 29...Kf7 30.Qg7+ Ke8 31.Qg8++. Milos-Teixeira, São Paulo Zonal, 20.9.2003.

4. 28.K×h7! K×h7 29.Rh1+ Kg6 (29...Kg8 30.Rh8++) 30.g8Q+ (1–0). 30...K×g8 31.Ne7++. Parligras-Vouldis, Athens, 2.9.2003.

5. 29...K×b3+! 30.c×b3 (30.Ka1 R×c2) 30...Nc1+ (0–1). 31.Ka1 Nb3++. Bologan-Bacrot, Enghien-les-Bains, 12.4.2001.

6. 27.K×g7+! K×g7 28.Qg5+ Kf7 29.Qf6+ (1–0). 29...Kg8 (29...Ke8 30.Rd8++) 30.Qg6+ Kh8 31.Rh3++. Rublevsky - Kalinin, Moscow (Aeroflot) 5.2.2002.

7. 35...Bb6+ 36.Kf1 (36.Kh1 Qh3++; 36.Kf3 Rf2++) 36...Qh3+! 37.K×e2 Qg2+ 38.Ke1 Qf2++. Hsago-micopo2001, Internet 2008.

8. 20.R×h7+! K×h7 21.Qh3+ Kg8 22.Rh1 Qd7 (22...R×f4 23.Qh8+ Kf7 24.Rh7+ Ke6 25.Q×d8) 23.Nf6+ (1–0). 23...K×f6 24.Qh8+ Kf7 25.Q×f6+ Kg8(e8) 26.Rh8++.

Roktim - Bandyopadhyay, Indian Championship, 18.12.2006.

9. 23.Kg7+! (1–0). 23...B×g7 (23...Kd8 24.R×f8+! R×f8 25.Qg5+ Rf6 26.Q×f6+ Ke8 27.Qe7++) 24.Rf7+ Kd8 25.Qg5+. Zude-Likavsky, Germany, 2007.

10. 22.Nd6+ B×d6 23.Bb5+ Kf8 24.Bh6+ Kg8 25.R×d6 f5 26.R×e6! Q×e6 27.Qg5+ (1–0). 27...Qg6 (27...Kf7 28.Qg7++) 28.Bc4+. Turov - Chebotarev, Russian Championship, Elista, 1.5.2001.

11. 24.R×e6+! (24.N×g7+ Kf7 25.N×e6) 24...B×e6 (24...Q×e6 25.N×g7+ and 26.N×e6) 25.Q×d8+ Kf7 26.Nh6+ g×h6 (26...Kg6 27.Q×h8 K×h6 28.B×f6 g×f6 29.Q×f6+ Kh5 30.g4+) 27.Q×f6+ (1–0). 27...Ke8 28.Rd8++; 27...Kg8 28.Qg7++. Tiviakov - Ermenkov, Struga, 16.9.2002.

12. 22.Re1! Q×b2 23.Ng5! Rad8? (23...Rfe8 24.N×e6! R×e6 25.Qh3! f5 26.Rh8+ Kf7 27.R×a8) 24.Rh8+! (1–0). 24...K×h8 25.Qh4+ Kg8 26.Qh7++. Mikhalevski-Formanek, Chicago, 30.5.2004.

13. 18.Nfg6! Bg5 19.Q×h5 Be3+ (19...Bh6 20.Ne7+) 20.Kf2 B×g6 21.N×g6 B×f2+ 22.Kh1! b×c4 23.Ne7++. Smirin-Kagansky, Israel Championship, Tel Aviv, 3.12.2002.

14. 22.R×f6+! R×f6 23.Q×h5+ Kf8 (23...Ke7 24.Bb4++) 24.Re3! Kf5 (24...a5 25.B×f6 Q×f6 26.Rf3) 25.Bb4+ Kg7 26.Rg3+ Kf6

27.Rg6+ Ke5 (27...Kf7 28.Qh7+ Ke8 29.Rg8+ Rf8 30.Rxf8+) **28.Qe2+ (1-0).** 28...Kd4 (28...Kf4 29.g3++) 29.c3++. Becerra-Sarkar, US Championship, San Diego, 11.3.2006.

15. **24.Re6! Rxf3** (24...fxe6 25.Bxe6+ Rf7 26.Qxg6+; 24...Rc7 25.Rfe1 fxe6 26.Bxe6+ Rff7 27.Qxg6+ Kf8 28.Qh6+ Kg8 29.Re5) **25.Kg2! Rf6 26.Rh1! Rxf2+ 27.Kg1!?** (27.Kxf2 fxe6+ 28.Kg2) **27...Qc7 28.Rxg6+! fxg6 29.Be6+ (1-0).** Bacrot-Van Mil, Bundesliga, 25.11.2001.

16. **18.Rxg7+! Nxg7** (18...Kxg7 19.Qh6+ Kg8 20.e5 exf5 21.Nxf5 f6 22.Bc4+ Rf7 23.Bxf7+ Kxf7 24.Qxh7+ Ng7 25.e6+ Kxe6 26.Nxg7+ Kf7 27.Nh5+ Ke8 28.Qg8+ 1-0, Odisharia-Javajishvili, Tiflis, 2002) **19.f6 Kh8 20.Bg5 Bxd4** (20...Nh5 21.e5 Rg8 22.Qxh5 Rg6 23.Bxg6 fxg6 24.Qh4 Qe8 25.Ne4) **21.fxg7+ Bxg7 22.e5 h6** (22...f5 23.exf6 Bh6 24.Bxh7!) **23.Qe4 f5 24.exf6 (1-0).** Haznedaroglu - Iotov, European Individual Championship, Anatolia, 24.5.2004.

2 - PIECE SACRIFICES

17. **26...Na2+! (0-1).** 27.Qxa2 Qc2++. Van Wely-L'Ami, Dutch Championship, Leeuwarden, 1.7.2004.

18. 15.Bxf7+! Kxf7 16.Qc4+ Ke8 17.Qe6+ Be7 18.Ng5 (1-0). Rejaibi-Drogou, Saint-Quentin, 20.4.2001.

19. **19.Ng5+! hxg5 20.Rh3++.**

Gustafsson-Buhmann, Bundesliga, 8.3.2003.

20. **23...Qxd6! 24.Qxd6 Ne2++.** Darbanvaighani - Paridar, Kish, 3.2.2005.

21. **45...Qb8+ 46.Kh1 Bxg2+! (0-1).** 47.Kxg2 Qg3+ 48.Kh1 Qg1++. I.Sokolov-Bologan, Poikovsky, 24.3.2006.

22. **17.Nxa7+!** **Kd7** (17...Bxa7?? 18.Qxc7++; 17...Kb8 18.Qxb6) **18.Qa4+ Ke7 19.d6+! cxd6** (19...Kf8 20.dxc7; 19...Rxd6 20.Bxd6+ cxd6 21.Rhe1+ Kf6 22.Qf4+) **20.Rhe1+ Kf6** (20...Kf8 21.Bxd6+ Kg8 22.Qe8+ Rxe8 23.Rxe8++) **21.Nd5+ (1-0).** 21...Kg6 22.Qe4+ f5 23.Qe6++. Shulman - Zimbeck, Minneapolis, 18.5.2005.

23. **22...Qb4+ 23.Ka1 Rc1+ 24.Rxc1 Rxc1+ 25.Ka2** (25.Qxc1 Bxc1) **25...Qc4+! 26.Kxa3 Ra1+ 27.Kb2 Qa2+ 28.Kc3 Qb3+ (0-1).** 29.Kd4 Qc4++. Epishin-Short, Malmo, 13.6.2002.

24. **25.Nd5! Qxd5** (25...Na3+ 26.Kc1; 25...Nd2+ 26.Kc1) **26.Bxc4 Qxc4 27.Qf6 (1-0).** 27...Qxa2+ 28.Kc1 Qa1+ 29.Kd2 Qa5+ 30.Ke2 d3+ 31.Kf3 Bd5+ 32.Kg3. Karjakin-Alekseev, Janty Mansysk, 2007.

25. **19.Nxd6! exd6 20.e7+ Kf7 21.Qxd6 Qe8 22.Bc5** (22.Rxb2 Qxe7 23.Qxe7 Rbxe7 24.Rxb8+) **22...Nd7 23.Qxc6 Rb8 24.Bxf7+ Kxf7** (24...Qxf7 25.Qxd7) **25.Qd5++.** Kristjansson-Neubauer, European Team Championship, Plovdiv, 20.10.2003.

26. 23...♗×h3!! 24.♕g5 (24.g×h3 ♘d3! 25.♘ce2 ♖×e2! 26.♕×e2 ♗f2+ 27.♔g2 ♕g3+ 28.♔h1 ♕×h3++) 24...♕×d4+! (0-1). 25.♖×d4 ♖e1++. Brandenburg-Postny, Hoogeveen, 23.10.2006.

27. 27.g6! ♕×h5 28.g×f7+ ♕×f7 29.♖h1 ♕f6 30.♖f2! ♕×d4 31.♖h8+! ♔×h8 32.♕h3+ ♔g8 33.♕×e6+ (1-0). 33...♔h8(h7) 34.♖h2++. Chudinovsky-Nikolenko, Moscow, 30.1.2007.

28. 22...♗h3! 23.g×h3 ♕×f3 24.♘c1 ♗×g3 25.h×g3 ♕×g3+ 26.♔h1 ♕×h3+ 27.♔g1 ♕g3+ 28.♔h1 ♖e6! 29.♘b3 g5! (0-1). 30.♕h2 ♖h6! 31.♕×h6 ♕g2++; 30.♖a2 ♖h6+ 31.♕h2 ♖×h2+ 32.♖×h4 ♘g4. Polzin - Shengelia, Austrian Team Championship, 18.1.2007.

29. 18.♕b3+! ♔g6 (18...♔f8 19.♘×f6 g×f6 20.♖e1 ♕c7 21.♕e3) 19.♘g5 ♖f8 (19...♔×g5? 20.♕f7; 19...♘d5 20.♗×d5 c×d5 21.♘f3) 20.♖e1 ♘d5 21.♗×d5 ♗×g5 (21...c×d5 22.♖×e7 ♔×g5 23.♖×g7+) 22.♗e6! ♗×e6 23.♖×e6+ ♗f6 24.♕d3+ ♔h6 (24...♔f7 25.♖×f6+ g×f6 26.♕×h7+ ♔e6 27.♖e1+) 25.♕f5 ♕d8 26.♗e3+ (1-0). Czebe-Hoang Thanh Trang, Budapest, 11.4.2002.

30. 1...♗h2+! 2.♔×h2 ♕f1 3.g×f3 (3.♔g3 f×g2) 3...♕×f2+ 4.♔h1 ♕×f3+ 5.♔h2 ♕f2+ 6.♔h1 ♕f1+ 7.♔h2 ♖f2+ 8.♔g3 ♖g2+ 9.♔h4 ♕f2+ 10.♔h5 g6+ 11.♔h6 ♕h4++. Casellas-Valido, Cuba, 2007.

31. 26...♘f4+ 27.♔h2 ♖g4! 28.e×f4 ♖dg8 29.♔h3 ♗f5 (29...♘d3) 30.♗e4 ♖g3+ (0-1).

Züger-Gyimesi, European Individual Championship, Ohrid, 1.6.2001.

32. 17.♕h7+ ♔f7 18.♘eg5+! f×g5 (18...♔e8 19.♗b5+) 19.♘e5+! ♔f6 20.♕×g6+ ♔×e5 21.♕e6+ ♔d4 22.♕e4++. Conquest-J.M.Degraeve, Clichy, 3.7.2001.

33. 27...♘d3! 28.♗×d3 ♗×g3! 29.♔h1 ♗×f2 30.♗f1 (30.♖g1 ♗×g1 31.♕×g1 f2+) 30...♕g1++. Shetty-Ramesh, Calcutta, 9.2.2001.

34. 28.♘f5+! g×f5 29.♕×f5 ♖fd8 30.♕×h7+ ♔f8 31.g6 ♖a7 32.g7+ ♔e7 33.♗g5+ ♔d7 34.♕f5+ ♔c6 35.♗e4+ (1-0). 35...♔c7 36.♗×d8+ ♔×d8 37.g8♕+ ♔c7 39.♕gc8++. A.Almeida-Gagunashvili, Chicago, 26.5.2007.

35. 20.♘×e5! f×e5 21.♕×e5+ ♔g8 (21...♔f7 22.♘g4 ♘d7 23.♘h6+ ♔f8 24.♕h8+ ♔e7 25.♕×h7+ ♔d6 26.♘f7+ ♔c7 27.♘×d8 ♖×d8 28.♕×g6) 22.♘g4 h5 23.♘h6+ ♔h7 24.♘f7 g5 (24...♘d7 25.♘g5+ ♔h6 26.♕e7) 25.♕h8+ ♔g6 26.♘e5++. Sulskis-Holmsten, Linares Open, 12.1.2001.

36. 22...e3! 23.f×e3 (23.♗×b7+ ♖×b7 24.h×g4 ♖×b2+ 25.♔f3 h×g4+ 26.♔g2 ♖dd2; 23.♗×e3 ♘×e3 24.f×e3 ♖d2+ 25.♔f3 g5) 23...♖d2+ 24.♔f3 ♖8d3 25.b4 ♗×e3 (25...♘×e3 26.b×c5 ♘×g2+ 27.♗e3 ♖×e3++) 26.♗×e3 g5 27.h×g4 h×g4++. Rodríguez Guerrero-Roiz. European Club Cup, Izmir, 8.10.2004.

37. 26.♗×f7+!! ♔×f7 27.♕a2+ ♔f8 (27...♔f6 28.♗d8+!! ♔e5 29.♘f3+ ♔f4 30.♕d2+ ♔g4 31.h3+ ♔h5 32.g4++) 28.♘e6+ ♖×e6 29.♕×e6 ♘e7 (29...♕g5 30.♖×d7

♗×d7 31.♗d6+ ♘e7 32.♕×d7)
**30.♖e3 ♔e8 31.♖f3 ♕h5 32.♗d6
(1–0).** 32...♕g5(h4) 33.♖f7.
Kramnik-Bruzón, Turin Olympiad,
3.6.2006.

38. **24.♘f6+!! g×f6** (24...♔f8
25.♕h8+! ♘×h8 26.♖×h8+ ♔e7
27.♖e8++) **25.g×f6 ♖×f4+ 26.♔e2!**
(26.♔e1? ♖h4) **26...♖f2+** (26...♖g4
27.♕h6! ♗f8 28.♕h7++) **27.♔×f2
♗×e3+ 28.♔f1!** (28.♔e1? ♗h6!
29.♕×h6 ♕×e5+) **(1–0).** Vuckovic-
Nestorovic, Belgrade, 23.1.2007.

39. **20.f5! g×f5 21.♘×f5! ♖g8**
(21...e×f5 22.♕×f5 0-0 23.♖ad1)
**22.♕f3 e×f5 23.♕×f5 ♖g7 24.e6
♘f6 25.♖ad1 ♕c7 26.♗e5 ♕b7
27.♗×f6 f×e6 28.♕h5+! ♖g6
29.♗×e7 ♕×e7** (29...♔×e7
30.♕×h7+ ♔e8 31.♕×g6+ ♔e7
32.♕f7++) **30.♕b5+ (1–0).** Van
Wely-Babula, Bundesliga, 24.4.2004.

40. **17...♘c2+! 18.♔d2** (18.♔f2
♖×c3 19.♘×g5 ♖×e3 20.♕×f7+
♔d8) **18...♘e4+ 19.♔×c2 ♗a4+
20.♔c1 (0–1).** 20...♖×c3+! 21.b×c3
♗a3+ 22.♖b2 ♕×b2++. Herráiz-
Shirov, Spanish Championship,
Ayamonte, 9.10.2002.

41. **23.f5! g×f5 24.♕g5+ ♔e8
25.♗×e6! ♖d2** (25...f×e6 26.♕g6+)
26.♗×f7+ ♔d7 (26...♔×f7
27.♕×f5+ ♔e8 28.♕e6+ ♔d8
29.♖×d2 c×d2 30.♘b6) **27.♕g7 ♖d8**
(27...♗×g2+ 28.♕×g2) **28.♗d5+ (1–
0).** 28...♔c8 29.♕×b7++. Volokitin-
Crisan, Portoroz, 3.7.2001.

42. **22.♗c2!!** (22.♕×g5+? ♘g6)
22...♔g7 (22...f5 23.♕×g5+ ♔f7
24.♗e4!, with the threat 25.♖c7+;
22...♖e8 23.♕×g5+ ♘g6 24.♕h6
♘f8 25.♖d4!; 22...♘g6 23.♗×g6

f×g6 24.♕×g6+ ♔h8 25.♖c7!)
23.b4!! (1–0). 23...♕b5 24.♕×g5+
♘g6 25.♕×b5; 23...♕×b4
24.♕×g5+ ♘g6 25.♗×g6 f×g6
26.♔c7+. Yakovich-Naiditsch,
Moscow (Aeroflot), 18.2.2007.

43. **27.♘g4! h×g4 28.♖×f7+ ♔g8
29.♕e4 ♗×b2+ 30.♔×b2 ♕c3+
31.♔b1 ♖h7 32.♖×7 (1–0).**
32...♔×h7 33.♕×g6+ ♔h8
34.♕h7++. Beliavsky - Postny,
European Individual Championship,
Warsaw, 26.6.2005.

44. **18.♘g5! h×g5** (18...♗×g5
19.♕h7+ ♔f7 20.♗×g5! h×g5
21.♖f3+) **19.h×g5 d×c3 20.♗f4**
(20.♖h8+ ♔f7 21.♕g6+ ♔e7
22.g×f6+ g×f6 23.♖h7+ ♔d6
24.♗f4+ ♔c6 25.♕e4+ ♔b6
26.♗c7+ ♕×c7 27.♖×c7 ♔×c7
28.♕×a8) **20...♔f7** (20...♗d4
21.♕g6!) **21.♕g6+ ♔e7 22.g×f6+
♖×f6 23.♕×g7+ ♖f7 24.♗g5+ ♔d6
25.♕×f7 ♕×g5 26.♖h7 ♕e5+**
(26...♕c1+ 27.♔e2 ♕d2+ 28.♔f3
♕d1+ 29.♔g2) **27.♔f1 ♔c6
28.♕e8+ ♔b6 29.♕d8+ ♔c6
30.♗e4+! (1–0).** 30...♕×e4
31.♕c7++. Topalov - Ponomariov,
Sofia, 21.5.2005.

45. **16.♘×f7! ♕b6?** (16...♔×f7
17.f×e6+ ♔×e6 18.♘f5! ♔f7 19.g4!
♔g8 20.♖de1 ♔f7 21.g5; 16...♔×f7
17.f×e6 ♔f8 18.e×d7 ♕×d7 19.d×c5)
**17.♖he1 c×d4 18.f×e6 ♕c7 19.♔b1!
♕×c2+ 20.♔a1 ♘b6 21.♘f5 ♘fd5
22.♕g4 ♗f6 23.♕g6 ♖×f7 24.e×f7+
(1–0).** 24...♔f8(h8) 25.♖e8+.
Efimenko - Epishin, Moscow
(Aeroflot), 23.2.2005.

46. **20.♗b8!! ♖a×b8 21.♕c7!
♖bd8** (21...♗f8 22.♕×d7 ♕f7
23.♕×c6 ♖ec8 24.♕a6 ♖×c3

25.♖e5; 21...♗f6 22.♕×d7 ♖×e3 23.♖×e3 f4 24.♖e6) **22.♖×e7 ♕g6** (22...♔f8 23.♕e5) **23.♖1e5 ♗c8 24.g4! ♔f8 25.♖×f5! ♗×f5 26.♗×f5 ♕h6 27.♖×h7 ♖c8 28.♗e6+ (1–0).** Palac-Atalik, Slovenian Team Championship, 20.11.2002.

47. **21...♘g4+ 22.♔g1** (22.h×g4 ♕h4+ 23.♔g1 ♗×f2+ 24.♔f1 ♖ae8 25.g3 ♗×g3) **22...♖e8! 23.♗d3** (23.♕×a7 ♖e1+ 24.♖×e1 ♕×e1+ 25.♖×e1 ♖×e1++; 23.h×g4 ♗×f2+ 24.♔f1 ♕h4) **23...♖e1+ 24.♗f1** (24.♖×e1 ♕×e1+ 25.♖×e1 ♖×e1+ 26.♗f1 ♗×f2+ 27.♔h1 ♖×f1++) **24...♕e2! (0–1).** 25.♖×e1 ♕×f2+ 26.♔h1 ♕g1++. Shkuran-Ivanchuk, Ukrainian Championship, Kharkov, 25.8.2004.

48. **20.♘g6+! ♔f7 21.♖f3+! ♔×g6** (21...♔g8 22.♘e7+) **22.♗d3+ ♔h5 23.♖h3+ ♔g4 24.f3+ ♔f4 25.♔f2! g4 26.g3+ (1–0).** 26...♔g5 27.f4++. Kasparov-Korchnoi, Zurich, 29.4.2001.

> ## 3 - VARIOUS SACRIFICES

49. **24.♕×h7+! (1–0).** 24...♔×h7 25.♔h3+. Vandevoort-Pira, Paris, 17.12.2003.

50. **24...♔×f3! 25.♔h2** (25.e×f3 ♕×f3) **25...♔×f2+! 26.♔×h3 ♕g2+ 27.♔g4 h5+ (0–1).** 28.♔h4 ♖e4+ 29.♔g5 ♕×g3++. Cabarkapa-Draghici, IBCA World Championship, Istanbul, 29.11.2002.

51. **39...d3! (0–1).** (a) 40.♗×d3 ♕d4+; (b) 40.♕×d3 ♘f4 41.♘f5 ♕c5; (c) 40.♖×a1 ♕d4+ 41.♔h1 ♕×a1+ 42.♖c1 d×e2 43.♖×a1 ♖f1+

44.♖×f1 e×f1♕++. Ehlvest-Shulman, Chicago, 28.5.2007.

52. **31.♔g8+! (1–0),** 31...♖×g8 32.♕f6+ ♖g7 33.♕×g7++; 31...♔×g8 32.♕g3+ ♔f7(h8) 33.♕g7++. A.Stefanova-M.Gurevich, Gibraltar, 2008.

53. **23.♗×g7! ♘×g7 24.♖d8 ♘ce6** (24...f6 25.♘h6+ ♔h8 26.♖×f8++) **25.♕×g7+! ♘×g7 26.♘h6+ (1–0).** 26...♔h8 27.♖×f8++. Zivanic-Ilincic, Belgrade, 28.6.2002.

54. **24...♕×a3+! 25.b×a3 ♔c2+ 26.♔b1 ♔d2+ 27.♔a1 ♘b3++.** Eriksson - Hellsten, Swedish Championship, Gothenburg, 11.7.2006.

55. **21...♖×e2! 22.♖×e2** (22.♗×e2 ♕×g3+ 23.♔g1 ♕h2+ 24.♔f1 ♕h1+ 25.♔f2 ♗g3+!; 22.♕×e2 ♕×g3+ 23.♔g1 ♕h2+ 24.♔f1 ♕h1+ 25.♔f2 ♗g3+ 26.♔e3 ♖e8+) **22...♕×g3+ 23.♔g1 ♗b6+ 24.♔f1 ♕h4! 25.♘d4 ♘×d4 26.c×d4 ♗×d4 27.♖d2 ♖e8 28.♗e4 ♗b5+ (0–1).** Langer-Atalik, Las Vegas, 26.7.2001.

56. **20...b4!! 21.b×c3 b×a3 22.♖d3?** (22.♖d5 ♗×d5 23.e×d5 a2+ 24.♔b2 a1♕+! 25.♕×a1 ♕b4+ 26.♔c1 ♗×c3 27.♕a2 ♗d2+! 28.♔d1 ♗f4 29.c4 ♕c3! 30.♗f1 ♕×f3+) **22...♕b4+! 23.c×b4** (23.♔a1 ♗×c3+ 24.♖×c3 ♕×c3+ 25.♔b1 a2++) **23...a2++.** Yaremko-Recuero, U16 World Championship, Herceg Novi, 18.9.2006.

57. **23.♖×g5! ♘×g5 24.♘f6 ♘×f3 25.♕×f3!** (25.♘×d7 ♘×e1 26.♕×f5 ♘e7 27.♕e4 c6 28.♘f6) **25...♕f7 26.♕×c6 ♔b8 27.♗h4 ♗b7 28.♘e4+ ♔c8 29.♘d6++.** Nataf-

Ostenstad, Calviá Olympiad, 18.10.2004.

58. 26.Q×e8! Bc3 (26...R×e8? 27.R×e8+ Kg7 28.Bf8+ Kg8 29.Bh6++) **27.Q×f7 (1–0).** Tzermiadianos - Oney, European Individual Championship, Istanbul, 11.6.2003.

59. 27.Qg7+! B×g7 28.h×g7+ K×h7 29.g8Q+ (1–0). 29...K×g8 30.K×h4++. Vachier Lagrave-David, ParBs, 23.12.2004.

60. 21.f5! Nh5?! (21...g×f5 22.Qg5 h5 23.Q×f5) **22.f×g6 B×c3+ 23.b×c3 Rf5** (23...h×g6 24.Qg5 Kh7 25.R×h5+ g×h5 26.Be4+ Kh8 27.Qh6+ Kg8 28.Qh7++) **24.Be4 Qb2 25.Rd1 Re5 26.0–0 R×e4** (26...h×g6 27.Qh6) **27.Qh6! h×g6 28.Rf7 (1–0).** Speelman-McDonald, British Championship, Torquay, 31.7.2002.

61. 22.N×f7! B×c2 (22...Q×f7 23.Qd8+ Ka7 24.Bd4+ b6 25.Q×b6+ Ka8 26.Q×a6+ Kb8 27.Be5+) **23.Q×c2 Q×f7 24.Be5+ Ka7 25.B×a6! b×a6** (25...K×a6 26.Qc4+ Ka5 27.Bc7+ b6 28.Qc6!) **26.Qc8 Qe8** (26...Qb7 27.Bd4+; 26...Nd7 27.Qc7+ Ka8 28.Bd4) **27.Bd4+ (1–0).** Korneev-Fernández Romero, Dos Hermanas, 30.3.2003.

62. 23.R×g5 Q×d3 24.B×e3 Q×c4 **25.f6! Re6** (25...B×d5 26.Q×d5+ Q×d5+ 27.R×d5 R×f6 28.Kg2; 25...R×f6 26.R×g7+! Kh8 27.Q×f6 Q×d5+ 28.Rg2++) **26.R×g7+ Kh8 27.R×h7+! (1–0).** 27...K×h7 28.Qh5+ Kg8 29.Qg6+ y 30.Qg7++. Nisipeanu - Babula, European Individual Championship, Warsaw, 21.6.2005.

63. 11.N×g4! N×g4 12.Q×g4 Q×b2 13.Nd2! Q×a1 14.Bb5 f5 15.Q×f5 Q×h1 16.Q×d7+ (1–0). 16...Kf7 17.Qe6++. Kozakov-Bolcan, European Club Cup, Chalkidiki, 26.9.2002.

64. 1...Qe2! 2.Kg5 (2.Qg1 Qf3!) 2...Qh5+ 3.Kf6 Qh8+ 4.Kg5 f6+! 5.e×f6 (5.B×f6) 5...Qh5++. Catelli-Dzhuraev, U18 World Championship, Turkey, 2007.

65. 47...Kg7!, with the unstoppable threat 48...Bh4+ 49.K×h4 Qh2+ 50.Kg5 Qh6++. He also won directly 47...Bh4+! Sopovavika-Pillsburyson, Internet, 2008.

66. 25.R×g7! K×g7 26.Qh6+ Kg8 (26...Kf7 27.Rb1 Q×c3 28.R×b7+ Ke8 29.Qe6+) **27.g6 h×g6 28.Q×g6+ Kh8 29.Kh1! Nf4** (29...Qb3 30.Q×h5+ Kg7 31.Rg1+ Kf6 32.Nd5+ c×d5 33.Rg6+ Ke7 34.Q×e5+) **30.Q×h5+ Kg8 31.Rg1+ Kf8 32.Qh8+ Kf7 33.Qg7+ (1–0).** 33...Ke8 (33...Ke6 34.Rg6+ Rf6 35.R×f6++) 34.Q×e5+ Kd8 35.Rg8+ Kd7 36.Rd7+. J.Polgár-Bareev, Candidates, Elista, 1.6.2007.

67. 18.B×f6!! e×f6 (18...Rf8 19.Qg3!) 19.Q×f6 Rg8 20.Rae1 d5 21.Qg5! Re7 22.Q×h6 Qa5 23.Rf6 Q×a2 24.R×g6 Rf8 25.Q×f8+! (1–0). 25...K×f8 26.Rf1+ Ke8 27.Rg8++. G.Jones-Van Wely, London, 17.8.2007.

68. 1.Q×g7+! Ke8 (1...R×g7?? 2.Rh8+) 2.Qg2! K×h3 3.Qg8+ Kd7 4.Q×f7+ Kc6 5.Q×e6+ Kc5 6.Rg5+ Kd4 7.Rd5+ (1–0). 7...K×c4 (7...Kc3 8.Q×h3+ K×c4 9.Qd3++) 8.Qe4+ Kc3 9.Qd4++. Nevednichy-

Kozul, Dresden, 2007.

69. 29.Qg6+! Nxg6 30.hxg6+ Kxg7 31.Bh6+ Kf6 32.Rdf1+ (1–0). Amonatov-Timofeev, Russian Championship, Moscow, 2007.

70. 22.Rxd4! cxd4 23.Qxd4 g5? (23...Rc8) 24.Rg3 Qf5 (24...Rh4? 25.Qxh4; 24...f6 25.exf6 Kf7 26.Re3 Qxf6 27.Be5 Qh6 28.Rf3+ Kg8 29.Bxh8 Qxh8 30.Qd5+ Kh7 31.Qxg5) 25.e6! f6 26.Rf3 Rh4 27.Qd1! Qg6 28.Qd5 Qe4 29.Rxf6! Qxd5 30.Rf8++. Yusupov-Kersten, German Championship, 23.11.2002.

71. 27...Nxg2!! 28.Kf1 (28.dxe7 Nxe1+ 29.Kf1 Ba6+ 30.Kxe1 Bc3+ 31.Qd2 Rg1++) 28...Nxe1 29.dxe7 Ba6+! 30.Bd3 (30.Kxe1 Bc3+, etc.) 30...Nxd3 31.Rxd3 (31.Qc6 Kxe7) 31...Bxd3+ 32.Ke1 Bc3+ (0–1). 33.Kd1 Rg1++. Lyaskovsky-Prohaszka, U14 World Championship, 11.9.2006.

72. 22.Qh5!! gxh5 (22...Kg8 23.Rxg6+! hxg6 24.Qxg6+ Kh8 25.Qh5+ Kg8 26.Ng4 Bg7 27.Ngh6+ Kh8 28.Nf7+ Kg8 29.Qg6) 23.Bd1! Bxd5 (23...Bg7 24.Rxg7+ Kf8 25.Bh6 Re7 26.Bxh5 Rxg7 27.Bxg7+ Kg8 28.Ng4 h6 29.Bg6) 24.exd5 (1–0). 24...Bg7 25.Rxg7+, etc. Zubarev-Lechtynsky, Pardubice, 26.7.2006.

73. 24...Rxh2!! 25.Kxh2 (25.Nxe4 Qh8 26.Ng3 Qh3; 25.f3 Qh8 26.fxe4 Rh1+ 27.Kf2 Qh2) 26...Qg7+! 27.Kh2 Qh6+ 28.Kg3 Qg5+ 29.Kh3 Bf5+ 30.Kh2 g1Q+! 31.Rxg1 Qh4+ 32.Kg2 Qh3++. Saidy-Becerra, Open USA, Phoenis, 8.8.2005.

74. 25.g5! Nxe5 26.dxe5 hxg5 (26...Bxg5 27.Bxg5 hx5 28.h6) 27.h6 Qxc4 28.hxg6 Kxg7 29.Bxg5!! Bxg5 30.Qf6+!! (1–0). 30...Bxf6 31.Kg3+ and mate in two. Apicella - Bauer, French Championship, Aix - les- Bains, 23.8.2003.

75. 16.Bxf6 Nxf6 17.Ng5! Ng4 (17...Bh6 18.Nxf7! Qxf7 19.e5 Ng4 20.Qd3 Bg7 21.exf6 Bxf6 22.Bb3) 18.Bb3! Ne3 19.Rxf7 Qxg3 20.hxg3 Nxd1 21.Re7+ (1–0). 21...Kh8 22.Rxh7++. Dvoiris-Bachin, Russian Championship, Elista, 30.4.2001.

76. 19...Rd8!! 20.Qxg7 Bf6! 21.Qxf6 Rg8! 22.Rg1 Rxd3 23.Bf2 Rd2! 24.Bg3 (24.Qh4 Bd5!) 24...Bd5! 25.Qh4 Qb7 26.h3 (26.Qh3 h4!) 26...Bxg2+ 27.Kh2 Bf1+ (0–1). Ulibin-Pia Cramling, Stockholm, 3.1.2005.

77. 23.Qg6!! Nb4 (23...hxg6? 24.hxg6+ Bh4 25.Rxh4++) 24.Rdg1! Bf8 (24...Nxd3+ 25.Kb1 Rg8 26.cxd3) 25.Nf6! Nxd3+ 26.Kb1 hxg6 27.hxg6+ Bxh1 28.Rxh1++. Smeets - Werle, Groningen, 21.12.2002.

78. 21.Qe8+! Kh7? (21...Nf8 22.Bf6!) 22.Nh5! (threat 23.Nf6+) 22...Be5 (22...Nxh4 23.Nf6+ gxf6 24.Rg1!; 22...Qc7 23.Rg1 Bxg1 24.Rxg1 Nf8 25.Be7) 23.Rg1 Nf4 24.Nxf4 Nxf3 (24...Bxf4 25.Qg6+; 24...Qc6 25.Qg6+ Kg8 26.Nd3) 25.Ng6 Qc6 26.Qh8++. Iuldachev-Gleizerov, Abu Dabi, 15.8.2002.

79. 23.Rhe1!! Qxd3 24.Rxe8+ Kf7 25.Rde1! Qe4 (25...Ne5 26.cxd3 Nxd3+ 27.Kc2 Nxe1+

28.♖×e1) **26.♘×e4 ♚×e8 27.♘×f6+ ♚f7** (27...♚d8 28.♖e8+ ♚c7 29.♘×h7; 27...♚f8 28.♖e8+ ♚f7 29.♘g5+ ♚×f6 30.♖e6++) **28.♘g5+ (1–0).** 28...♚×f6 29.♖e6++; 28...♚f8 29.♖e8++. Naiditsch-Koneru, Wijk aan Zee, 20.1.2003.

80. **26.♔f2!** (threat 27.♖h1) **26...e4** (26...h5 27.♕f5) **27.♗×e4 h5** (27...♚×e4 28.♕×e4 ♖e8 29.♕f5) **28.♕f5! ♚f8** (28...♚×e4 29.♕h7+ ♚e8 30.♕×e4+) **29.♕h7 ♚×e4 30.♕h8+ (1–0).** 30...♚f7 31.♘h6+ ♚g6 32.♕g7++. Vaiser - J.M.Degraeve, French Championship, Val-d'Isère, 19.8.2004.

4 - QUEEN AND MULTIPLE SACRIFICES

81. **28.♔×f5! e×f5 29.♔h8+! (1–0).** 29...♚×h8 30.♕h4(h3, h5)+ ♚g8 31.♕h7++. Eljanov-Wang Yue, Moscow (Aeroflot), 21.2.2005.

82. **1.♖dd7! ♘×d7 2.♕×a6+! (1–0).** 2...b×a6 3.♖a7++. Reinaldo-Caselas, Sanxenxo, 2007.

83. **38.♕×f7+! (1–0).** 38...♚×f7 39.♖e8++. Bellón-Suba, Calviá, 18.10.2007.

84. **50.♖g×h5+! g×h5 51.♖×h5+! ♕×h5 52.♕g7++.** Nijboer-Van Delft, Dieren, 26.7.2007.

85. **23...♘fg4+! 24.h×g4** (24.♔h1 ♘f3! 25.♗×g7 ♘ge5 26.♗b1 ♚×g7 27.♗×e4 ♚f6) **24...♖h6+ 25.♔g1 ♘f3+! 26.g×f3 e×f3 (0–1).** Henrichs-Prusikin, German Championship, 23.1.2007.

86. **29...♖×f3! 30.g×f3** (30.♗×f3 ♗×f3 31.g×f3 d1♕) **30...♖×d1! (0–1).** 30...♖×d1 31.♖×d1 ♗×f3+ 32.♕g2 ♕e1+ 33.♖×e1 d×e1♕++. Kristjansson-Caruana, Reikiavik, 7.3.2008.

87. **21...♖×c2!! 22.♘×c2 ♗c4 23.b3?** (23.♘×b4! ♕×b4 24.♖d4 ♕a4 25.♖×c4 ♘×c4 26.b3 ♖b8 27.♗d4) **23...♗×b3 24.a×b3 ♕×b3+ 25.♔c1 ♕a2! 26.♖d3 b3 27.♔d1 b×c2+ 28.♔c1 ♕a1+ 29.♔d2 ♕×h1 30.♔e2** (30.♗×h1 c1♕+ 31.♔e2 ♕×h1) **30...c1♕ (0–1)** Shomoev-Potkin, European Individual Championship, Dresden, 6.4.2007.

88. **23.e7! ♕b6** (23...♗×e7 24.♖×e7 ♘×e7 25.♖×e7 ♖ad8 26.♕d4 ♘f6 27.♕h4+) **24.e×f8♕+ ♘×f8 25.♖e6! ♘×e6 26.♖×e6 ♘f6 27.♗×g5+ ♚×g5** (27...♚g7 28.♖×f6 ♗×f6 29.♕d7+) **28.♕d2+ (1–0).** Carlsen-Radjabov, Biel, 2.8.2007.

89. **23.♘f6!! g×f6 24.♕h6+ ♚g8 25.e×f6 ♖e8 26.♗f4 ♖c8 27.♗d6! ♘cd4 28.♕g7+!! (1–0).** 28...♘×g7 29.♘h6++. Adly-Laznicka, World Youth Championship, Kemer, 11.10.2007.

90. **45...♗g2+! 46.♔×g2 ♕×g3+ 47.♔f1** (47.♔h1 ♕h3+ 48.♕h2 ♖e1+ 49.♖×e1 ♖×e1++) **47...♕h3+ 48.♕g2 ♘g3+ (0–1).** 49.f×g3 ♕×g2++; 49.♔g1 ♖e1+, etc. Inarkiev-Kamsky, World Cup, Bakú, 21.4.2008.

91. **23...♖e2! 24.♖×e2 ♕h3 25.♘e3** (25.♕×f3 ♖×f3 26.♘×d6 ♘f6! 27.♖ae1 h6) **25...♖f4!! (0–1).** 26.♕×a6 (26.g×f4?? ♗×f4) 26...♖h4 27.♕a8+ ♚f7 28.♕e8+ ♚×e8 29.♘g2+ f×e2 30.♘×h4 ♗b4. Naiditsch-Gustafsson, European

Individual Championship, Dresden, 11.4.2007.

92. 54.R×f7! Q×f7 (54...K×f7?? 55.N×e5+ B×e5 56.Q×d7+) **55.N×e5! Rg2+** (55...B×e5?? 56.Qc8++) **56.Ke3 Qf4+ 57.K×f4 B×e5+ 58.Ke3 K8g7 59.dc8+ Kf7 60.de6+ Kf8 61.Rf5+ (1-0).** Bercys-Simutowe, Chicago, 28.5.2007.

93. 26...B×a3! 27.b×a3 R×a3+! **28.K×a3 Qb4+ 29.Ka2 Ra8+ 30.Na4 c3!** (30...R×a4+ 31.Q×a4 Q×a4+ 32.Kb1 c3 33.Rc2 Nh3) **31.Ka1 c×d2 32.Na2 R×a4 33.g×f4 Qd4+ 34.Kb1 Rc4 35.Qb3 f×e4 36.d6 c×d6 37.f×e4 Q×e4+ 38.Kb2 Q×h1! 39.Q×c4+ Kg7 40.Qe6** (40.Nc3 Qc1+ 41.Kb3 d1Q+ 42.N×d1 Q×d1) **40...d1N+!** (40...d1Q? 41.Qe7+, draw) **41.Kc2 Ne3+ 42.Kd3 Nf5 ...** 54 moves. **(0-1).** Wang Yue-Cheparinov, World Cup, Janty Mansysk, 4.12.2007.

94. 16.B×h6! g×h6 17.Rh3 R×c4 **18.N×c4 Kg7 19.Qg3+ Kh7 20.Qd3+ Kg7 21.Nd6 Qb8 22.R×e6! f×e6 23.Rg3+ Ng4 24.R×g4+ Kf6 25.Qh7 (1-0).** Onischuk-Vescovi, Pokovsky, 20.4.2002.

95. 21.Rg3! f5 (21...N×c6 22.N×g7 N×d4 23.N×e8 Ne2+ 24.Q×e2 Q×e8 25.Qe5+; 21...e5 22.Q×c8 R×c8 23.N×e5) **22.Qh4! N×c6 23.Nf6! h6 24.Q×h6+! g×h6 25.Kg8++.** Karpov-M.Stojanovic, Valjevo, 20.6.2007.

96. 15.Nc×d5! e×d5 16.R×d5 Nd4 (16...N×d5? 17.Ne6+) **17.R×d7! N×f3** (17.N×d7? 18.Ne6+ Kg8 19.B×e7 N×f3 20.N×d8 Nfe5 21.f4) **18.R×d8+ B×d8 19.g×f3 Ke7**

20.Bc4 Re8 21.Re1+ (21.Ne6!) 21...Kd7 22.Rd1+ Kc8 23.Ne6 Ra7 24.N×d8 h6 (24...R×d8 25.Be6+) ...38 moves. **(1-0).** Fernández Barrera-Lariño, La Roda, 22.3.2008.

97. 25.Qd3! Nf5 26.N×e6! B×e6 27.K×f5 B×f5 28.Q×f5 Kfe8 **29.Qh7+ Kf8 30.Qh8+ (1-0).** 30...Ke7 31.Q×g7+! B×g7 32.Kf7+ Ke6 33.Bf5++. Garbisu-Kosic, Budapest, 7.3.2008.

98. 34...Nh3+ 35.g×h3 g×h3+ **36.Bg3 Q×e4 37.Qc3** (37.Qb6 h4; 37.Qc4 Qe3+ 38.Kh1 Bg4) **37...Q×f1+! 38.K×f1 Bb5+ (0-1).** 39.Kf2 Qg2+ 40.Ke3 Qe2++. Pavlov-Zajarevich, Russia, 2005.

99. 16.R×h7! K×h7 17.Qh5+ Kg8 18.N×g6! f×g6 19.Qh8+ Kf7 **20.Qh7+ Bg7 21.B×g7 e5** (21...N×g7 22.B×g6+ Kf8 23.Qh8++) **22.Q×g6+ Kg8 23.Qh7+ Kf7 24.Bh6+ (1-0).** 24...Ke6 25.Qg6+ Nf6 26.Q×f6++; 24...Ng7 25.Q×g7+ Ke8 26.Qf8++. Oral-Navara, Czech Championship, Luhacovice, 25.2.2003.

100. 20.R×f6! b×c3 (20...B×f6 21.B×f6 Re6 22.g5 h5 23.Nd5) **21.R×f7! K×f7 22.Bc4+ d5 23.e×d5 Red8 24.d×c6+ Ke8 25.Bf7+! K×f7 26.Q×h7+ Ke6 27.Qg6+ (1-0).** Berg-Buhr, Bundesliga, 25.11.2001.

101. 1.B×h6+! K×h6 2.Ng5! b5 3.N×e6+ Kh7 4.Qg5! Ng8 5.R×a4! b×a4 6.h5! (1-0). 6...g×h5 7.B×f5+ Kh8 8.Rb8+; 6...R×h5 7.Nf8+ Kg7 8.Q×g6+ K×f8 9.Rb8+ Ke7 10.Qe8++; 6...Rg7 7.h×g6+ Kh8 8.N×g7 K×g7 9.Rb7+. Becerra-A.López, Miami, 2007.

102. 41...Q×f4! 42.b×c6 Qf3!! 43.c×b7+ Kf5 (0–1). There is no defense against ...Rh1+. Kramnik-Anand, Melody Amber (rapid), Nice, 15.3.2008.

103. 22.Re8! Q×e8 (22...Ng5 23.Q×f6+! Q×f6 24.B×f6+ K×f6 25.R×a8; 22...Ne5 23.B×e5 Q×e8 24.Q×f6 Kg8 25.Qh8+ Kf7 26.Q×h7+ Ke6 27.B×g6 Qe7 28.Qh5) 23.Q×f6+ Kg8 24.B×g6! (1–0). 24...h×g6 25.Q×g6+ Bg7 26.Q×g7++; 24...Qe6 25.B×f7+ Q×f7 26.Qh8++. Kinslinsky-Berlin, Minsk, 16.7.2006.

104. 23...Bh4! 24.Q×h4? (24.Rd2 Q×f3 25.Q×f3 B×f3 26.g3) 24...R×g2+!! 25.R×g2 R×g2+ 26.Kf1 (26.K×g2 Q×f3+ 27.Kg1 Qg2++) 26...Q×f3+ (0–1). 27.Bf2 Rg1+! 28.K×g1 Qg2++. J.M.Degraeve-Guidarelli, French Championship, Aix - les -Bains, 19.8.2003.

105. 20...Qf4! (threatens 21...Bd6) 21.Qc1 (21.B×h3 Bd6) 21...N×f2+ 22.Kg1 Nf3+! 23.Kf2 (23.B×f3 Qg3+ 24.Bg2 Nh3+ 25.Kh1 Bd6) 23...Bc5+ 24.Ke2 R×b2+ 25.Q×b2 Qe3+ 26.Kd1 Qd3+ (0–1). 27.Kc1 Be3+. Sivojo-Popov, St. Petersburg Championship, 21.4.2001.

106. 27...N×g4! 28.f×g4 N×d4! 29.N×d4 Re1 30.Ncb5 (30.Nde2 R×f1+! 31.K×f1 Q×h2) 30...Qg3+ 31.Rg2 (31.Qg2 R×f1+ 32.K×f1 Re1++) 31...B×d4+! (0–1). 32.Q×d4 (32.N×d4 R×f1++) 32...R×f1+ 33.K×f1 Re1++ (33...Qe1++). Panczyk - Akesson, Cappelle-la-Grande, 20.2.2006.

107. 22...N×c3 (22...R×h4!) 23.Ba3 (23.Q×c3 R×h4 24.Ba3 Qg5) 23...R×h4! 24.g×h4 (24.B×e7 Rh1+ 25.Kf2 Ne4+ 26.Ke1 R×f1+ 27.K×f1 N×d2+) 24...Q×h4 25.Qh2 g3! (0–1). 26.Q×h4 Ne2++. Saiboulatov - Michiels, Belgian Championship, Eupen, 5.7.2003.

108. 20.Rf6!! Rfd8 (20...c4 21.Qh5 c×d3 22.Rg3; 20...g×f6 21.Qg3+ Kh8 22.Qh4; 20...Rfe8 21.Qh5 Qe7 22.Rg3) 21.Qh5 Rf8 22.Rg3 c4 23.R×g7! c×d3 (23...K×g7 24.Q×h6+ Kg8 25.Qh7+ Kf8 26.Qh8++) 24.Rg8+! K×g8 25.R×h6 (1–0). Gashimov-Lalic, Cappelle-la-Grande, 9.3.2007.

109. 21...Q×f2+!! 22.K×f2 Bc5+ 23.Kf3 (23.Bd4 B×d4+ 24.Kf3 Rf6+ 25.Kg4) 23...R×f6+ 24.Kg4 Ne5+ 25.Kg5 (25.R×e5 Bc8+! 26.Kh4 R×e5) 25...Rg6+ 26.Kh5 f6 27.R×e5 R×e5+ 28.Kh4 Bc8 (0–1). 29.Bd5+ (29.g4 Bf2+ 30.Kh3 Rh6++) 29...R×d5 30.g4 Rd3, and mate in a few. Krasenkow-Nakamura, Barcelona (Casino), 19.10.2007.

110. 22.Bf6!! g×f6 23.Qh6 Nac5 (23...Bb7 24.Q×f6 Nac5 25.Nh6+ Kf8 26.B×e6! N×e6 27.Nf5 Kg8 28.R×e6 f×e6 29.Nh6++) 24.Rbd1! Qb7 (24...Qc7 25.Rd4 Ne4 26.Re×e4 d×e4 27.R×e4) 25.Rd4 Ne4 26.Re×e4! d×e4 27.Q×f6 Qc7 28.Nh6+ Kf8 29.Qh8+ Ke7 30.Nf5++. Sandipan-Tiviakov, Ottawa, 14.7.2007.

111. 16.Bf6! Nf4+ 17.Kd2! (17.Q×f4? e5, followed by 18...Qa6+! Y 19...Q×f6) 17...Ng6 18.h×g6 f×g6 (18...h×g6 19.Rah1 and mate) 19.R×h7! (1–0). 19...K×h7 20.Rh1+ Kg8 21.Q×g6.

Individual Championship, Dresden, 11.4.2007.

92. 54.♜×f7! ♛×f7 (54...♚×f7?? 55.♞×e5+ ♝×e5 56.♛×d7+) **55.♞×e5! ♜g2+** (55...♝×e5?? **56.♛c8++) 56.♚e3 ♛f4+ 57.♚×f4 ♝×e5+ 58.♚e3 ♚g7 59.dc8+ ♚f7 60.de6+ ♚f8 61.♜f5+ (1-0).** Bercys-Simutowe, Chicago, 28.5.2007.

93. 26...♝×a3! 27.b×a3 ♜×a3+! **28.♚×a3 ♛b4+ 29.♚a2 ♜a8+ 30.♞a4 c3!** (30...♜×a4+ 31.♛×a4 ♛×a4+ 32.♚b1 c3 33.♜c2 ♞h3) **31.♚a1 c×d2 32.♞a2 ♜×a4 33.g×f4 ♛d4+ 34.♚b1 ♜c4 35.♛b3 f×e4 36.d6 c×d6 37.f×e4 ♛×e4+ 38.♚b2 ♛×h1! 39.♛×c4+ ♚g7 40.♛e6** (40.♞c3 ♛c1+ 41.♚b3 d1♛+ 42.♞×d1 ♛×d1) **40...d1♞+!** (40...d1♛? 41.♛e7+, draw) **41.♚c2 ♞e3+ 42.♚d3 ♞f5** ... 54 moves. **(0-1).** Wang Yue-Cheparinov, World Cup, Janty Mansysk, 4.12.2007.

94. 16.♝×h6! g×h6 17.♜h3 ♜×c4 **18.♞×c4 ♚g7 19.♛g3+ ♚h7 20.♛d3+ ♚g7 21.♞d6 ♛b8 22.♜×e6! f×e6 23.♜g3+ ♞g4 24.♜×g4+ ♚f6 25.♛h7 (1-0).** Onischuk-Vescovi, Pokovsky, 20.4.2002.

95. 21.♜g3! f5 (21...♞×c6 22.♞×g7 ♞×d4 23.♞×e8 ♞e2+ 24.♛×e2 ♛×e8 25.♛e5+; 21...e5 22.♛×c8 ♜×c8 23.♞×e5) **22.♛h4! ♞×c6 23.♞f6! h6 24.♛×h6+! g×h6 25.♚g8++.** Karpov-M.Stojanovic, Valjevo, 20.6.2007.

96. 15.♞c×d5! e×d5 16.♜×d5 ♞d4 (16...♞×d5? 17.♞e6+) **17.♜×d7! ♞×f3** (17.♞×d7? 18.♞e6+ ♚g8 19.♝×e7 ♞×f3 20.♞×d8 ♞fe5 21.f4) **18.♜×d8+ ♝×d8 19.g×f3 ♚e7**

20.♝c4 ♜e8 21.♜e1+ (21.♞e6!) **21...♚d7 22.♜d1+ ♚c8 23.♞e6 ♜a7 24.♞×d8 h6** (24...♜×d8 25.♝e6+) ...38 moves. **(1-0).** Fernández Barrera-Lariño, La Roda, 22.3.2008.

97. 25.♛d3! ♞f5 26.♞×e6! ♝×e6 27.♚×f5 ♝×f5 28.♛×f5 ♚fe8 **29.♛h7+ ♚f8 30.♛h8+ (1-0).** 30...♚e7 31.♛×g7+! ♝×g7 32.♚f7+ ♚e6 33.♝f5++. Garbisu-Kosic, Budapest, 7.3.2008.

98. 34...♞h3+ 35.g×h3 g×h3+ **36.♝g3 ♛×e4 37.♛c3** (37.♛b6 h4; 37.♛c4 ♛e3+ 38.♚h1 ♝g4) **37...♚×f1+! 38.♚×f1 ♝b5+ (0-1).** 39.♚f2 ♛g2+ 40.♚e3 ♛e2++. Pavlov-Zajarevich, Russia, 2005.

99. 16.♜×h7! ♚×h7 17.♛h5+ ♚g8 18.♞×g6! f×g6 19.♛h8+ ♚f7 **20.♛h7+ ♚g7 21.♝×g7 e5** (21...♞×g7 22.♝×g6+ ♚f8 23.♛h8++) **22.♛×g6+ ♚g8 23.♛h7+ ♚f7 24.♝h6+ (1-0).** 24...♚e6 25.♛g6+ ♞f6 26.♛×f6++; 24...♞g7 25.♛×g7+ ♚e8 26.♛f8++. Oral-Navara, Czech Championship, Luhacovice, 25.2.2003.

100. 20.♜×f6! b×c3 (20...♝×f6 21.♝×f6 ♜e6 22.g5 h5 23.♞d5) **21.♜×f7! ♚×f7 22.♝c4+ d5 23.e×d5 ♜ed8 24.d×c6+ ♚e8 25.♝f7+! ♚×f7 26.♛×h7+ ♚e6 27.♛×g6+ (1-0).** Berg-Buhr, Bundesliga, 25.11.2001.

101. 1.♝×h6+! ♚×h6 2.♞g5! b5 3.♞×e6+ ♚h7 4.♛g5! ♞g8 5.♜×a4! **b×a4 6.h5! (1-0).** 6...g×h5 7.♝×f5+ ♚h8 8.♜b8+; 6...♜×h5 7.♞f8+ ♚g7 8.♛×g6+ ♚×f8 9.♜b8+ ♚e7 10.♛e8++; 6...♜g7 7.h×g6+ ♚h8 8.♞×g7 ♚×g7 9.♜b7+. Becerra-A.López, Miami, 2007.

102. **41...Q×f4! 42.b×c6 Qf3!! 43.c×b7+ Kf5 (0–1).** There is no defense against ...Rh1+. Kramnik-Anand, Melody Amber (rapid), Nice, 15.3.2008.

103. **22.Re8! Q×e8** (22...Ng5 23.Q×f6+! Q×f6 24.B×f6+ K×f6 25.R×a8; 22...Ne5 23.B×e5 Q×e8 24.Q×f6 Kg8 25.Qh8+ Kf7 26.Q×h7+ Ke6 27.B×g6 Qe7 28.Qh5) **23.Q×f6+ Kg8 24.B×g6! (1–0).** 24...h×g6 25.Q×g6+ Bg7 26.Q×g7++; 24...Qe6 25.B×f7+ Q×f7 26.Qh8++. Kinslinsky-Berlin, Minsk, 16.7.2006.

104. **23...Bh4! 24.Q×h4?** (24.Rd2 Q×f3 25.Q×f3 B×f3 26.g3) **24...R×g2+!! 25.R×g2 R×g2+ 26.Kf1** (26.K×g2 Q×f3+ 27.Kg1 Qg2++) **26...Q×f3+ (0–1).** 27.Bf2 Rg1+! 28.K×g1 Qg2++. J.M.Degraeve-Guidarelli, French Championship, Aix - les -Bains, 19.8.2003.

105. **20...Qf4!** (threatens 21...Bd6) **21.Qc1** (21.B×h3 Bd6) **21...N×f2+ 22.Kg1 Nf3+! 23.Kf2** (23.B×f3 Qg3+ 24.Bg2 Nh3+ 25.Kh1 Bd6) **23...Bc5+ 24.Ke2 R×b2+ 25.Q×b2 Qe3+ 26.Kd1 Qd3+ (0–1).** 27.Kc1 Be3+. Sivojo-Popov, St. Petersburg Championship, 21.4.2001.

106. **27...N×g4! 28.f×g4 N×d4! 29.N×d4 Re1 30.Ncb5** (30.Nde2 R×f1+! 31.K×f1 Q×h2) **30...Qg3+ 31.Rg2** (31.Qg2 R×f1+ 32.Q×f1 Re1++) **31...B×d4+! (0–1).** 32.Q×d4 (32.N×d4 R×f1++) 32...R×f1+ 33.K×f1 Re1++ (33...Qe1++). Panczyk - Akesson, Cappelle-la-Grande, 20.2.2006.

107. **22...N×c3** (22...R×h4!) **23.Ba3** (23.Q×c3 R×h4 24.Ba3 Qg5) **23...R×h4! 24.g×h4** (24.B×e7 Rh1+ 25.Kf2 Ne4+ 26.Ke1 R×f1+ 27.K×f1 N×d2+) **24...Q×h4 25.Qh2 g3! (0–1).** 26.Q×h4 Ne2++. Saiboulatov - Michiels, Belgian Championship, Eupen, 5.7.2003.

108. **20.Rf6!! Rfd8** (20...c4 21.Qh5 c×d3 22.Rg3; 20...g×f6 21.Qg3+ Kh8 22.Qh4; 20...Rfe8 21.Qh5 Qe7 22.Rg3) **21.Qh5 Rf8 22.Rg3 c4 23.R×g7! c×d3** (23...K×g7 24.Q×h6+ Kg8 25.Qh7+ Kf8 26.Qh8++) **24.Rg8+! K×g8 25.R×h6 (1–0).** Gashimov-Lalic, Cappelle-la-Grande, 9.3.2007.

109. **21...Q×f2+!! 22.K×f2 Bc5+ 23.Kf3** (23.Bd4 B×d4+ 24.Kf3 Rf6+ 25.Kg4) **23...R×f6+ 24.Kg4 Ne5+ 25.Kg5** (25.R×e5 Bc8+! 26.Kh4 R×e5) **25...Rg6+ 26.Kh5 f6 27.R×e5 R×e5+ 28.Kh4 Bc8 (0–1).** 29.Bd5+ (29.g4 Bf2+ 30.Kh3 Rh6++) 29...R×d5 30.g4 Rd3, and mate in a few. Krasenkow-Nakamura, Barcelona (Casino), 19.10.2007.

110. **22.Bf6!! g×f6 23.Qh6 Nac5** (23...Bb7 24.Q×f6 Nac5 25.Nh6+ Kf8 26.B×e6! N×e6 27.Nf5 Kg8 28.R×e6 f×e6 29.Nh6++) **24.Rbd1! Qb7** (24...Qc7 25.Rd4 Ne4 26.Re×e4 d×e4 27.R×e4) **25.Rd4 Ne4 26.Re×e4! d×e4 27.Q×f6 Qc7 28.Nh6+ Kf8 29.Qh8+ Ke7 30.Nf5++.** Sandipan-Tiviakov, Ottawa, 14.7.2007.

111. **16.Bf6! Nf4+ 17.Kd2!** (17.Q×f4? e5, followed by 18...Qa6+! Y 19...Q×f6) **17...Ng6 18.h×g6 f×g6** (18...h×g6 19.Rah1 and mate) **19.R×h7! (1–0).** 19...K×h7 20.Rh1+ Kg8 21.Q×g6.

Bologan-Vaganian, European Club Cup, 12.10.2006.

112. **21.Nd5! e×d5** (21...Qd8 22.Nf6+!) **22.e×d5 R×c2 23.g6 h×g6** (23...f×g6 24.Qe6+ Kf8 25.h×g6 Bf6 26.g×h7) **24.h×g6 Rf8 25.g×f7+ R×f7 26.B×g7! R×g7 27.Qe6+ Kh8** (27...Kf8 28.R×g7!) **28.R×g7! K×g7 29.Rg1+ (1-0).** 29...Kh7 30.Qg6+ Kh8 31.Qh6++. Ivanchuk-Van Wely, Montecarlo (blindfold) 20.3.2006.

113. **25...Bf4! 26.Kf3 Be5! 27.K×g4 Rd3! 28.Raf1 f6! 29.Bf3 Bd7+ 30.Kh4 h5 31.Rhg1 g5+ 32.R×g5+** (32.K×h5 Kf7 y 33...Rh8++) **32...f×g5+ 33.K×g5?** (33.K×h5 Bf4) **33...Kh7! 34.Nd5 Rg8+ 35.Kh4 R×d5! (0-1).** 36.e×d5 Bf6+ 37.K×h5 Be8++. Esen-Golubev, Moscow (Aeroflot), 13.2.2006.

114. **21.B×h7+! K×h7 22.Ne4 Qe5 23.Rh4+ Kg8 24.Bf4 d3** (24...Qd5 25.Bh6 f5 26.B×g7 K×g7 27.Qh5; 24...Qb5 25.Qg4 f5 26.Qg6 f×e4 27.Qh7+ Kf7 28.Bd6+) **25.B×e5 d×e2 26.Nf6+! (1-0).** 26...B×f6 27.B×f6 e×f1Q+ 28.K×f1, and mate on h8 follows. Short-Zhukova, Gibraltar, 28.1.2006.

115. **18.Rd×d5! B×d5** (18...Bd6, 18...Qc7) **19.Ba4+! Ke7 20.Bc5+ Ke6 21.e×d5+ K×f5 22.Bc2+ Kg5 23.Qe3+ Nf4 24.Qg3+ Kh5 25.Bd1+ (1-0).** Langrock-Reddmann, Hamburg, 21.10.2001.

116. **23...Nf4+ 24.g×f4 Kg6+ 25.Kh1 Qh3+ 26.Rh2 Q×h2+! 27.K×h2 Kf7! (0-1).** Then ...Rh8+. Neiksans - Stefansson, Liepaja, 1.8.2004.

117. **28.B×h6!! R×f5** (28...g×h6 29.Qf4 Rg5 30.Nd4) **29.g×f5 Kh7** (29...g6 30.f×g6+; 29...Rc8 30.R×g7+ Kf8 31.Rg2+ Ke8 32.Rg8+ Ke7 33.f6+ N×f6 34.R×c8 Q×c8 35.Bg5) **30.B×g7 Rg8 31.Rfg1 Qd8** (31...Ne5 32.h6 Nf3 33.Rf1 Ne5 34.Rg3) **32.Nd2 Nc5** (32...Nf6 33.h6 Qe7 34.e5! Q×e5 35.Nf3 Q×f5 36.Ng5+ Kg6 37.Ne4+) **33.f6 Qe8** (33...Rh8 34.Rg4 Nd7 35.Nf3 N×f6 36.Ng5+ K×g7 37.Ne6+ Kh6 38.N×d8) **34.Rg6! (1-0).** 34...R×g7 (34...f×g6 35.h×g6+ Q×g6 36.Rh1+) 35.R×g7+ Kh8 36.h6 Qd8 37.R×f7. Motylev-Obolenskij, Kazán, 4.9.2005.

118. **30.R×g6! R×g6 31.B×c4 Ke7 32.Rb7+ Kd6 33.Qh5! B×c4 34.Ne4+! (1-0).** 34...f×e4 (34...Kd5 35.Q×f5++) 35.Qe5++. Beliavsky-Mamedyarov, Spanish Team Championship, 2.9.2005.

119. **20...R×g2! 21.K×g2 B×e4+ 22.Kh2** (22.Kg1 Nf3+) **22...Nf3+ 23.Kg2** (23.R×f3 B×f3 24.Nac1 Kd7) **23...Kd7 24.Rf2** (24.R×f3 Rg8+ 25.Kf2 Bh4+) **24...Rg8+ 25.Kf1 Bh4 26.N×b4 d5! 27.N×a6 Rg1+!** (27...Qh2!? 28.R×h2 N×h2++) **28.N×g1 Ng3+ (0-1).** 29.Kg2 Ne1+ 30.Kh2 Nf1++. Petkovski-Timoshenko, European Individual Championships, Ohrid, 1.6.2001.

120. **18.Ng6! f×g6?** (18...Rfe8 19.N×e7+ R×e7 20.d×c5) **19.Q×e6+ Kh8 20.h×g6! Ng8 21.Bh6! g×h6 22.R×h6+! N×h6 23.Q×e7 Nf7 24.g×f7! Kg7** (24...Qb6 25.Qe5+ Kh7 26.Rh1+) **25.Rd3 Rd6** (25...Qb6 26.Rg3+ Rg6 27.R×g6+ K×g6 28.d5) **26.Rg3+ Rg6 27.Qe5+ K×f7 28.Qf5+ Rf6** (28...Ke7

29.Re3+) **29.Qd7++**. Carlsen-Ernst, Wijk aan Zee, 24.1.2004.

121. **23.Nxe6!! f×e6 24.Q×e6 Rd7** (24...Rd8 25.Rg3) **25.Rg3 Qf8 26.Re1! Raa7** (26...Rg7 27.R×g7 ♔×g7 28.Qg4+ ♔h8 29.Qd4+ ♔g8 30.Qd5+) **27.Qf6+!** **(1–0)**. 27...Q×f6 28.Re8+. Topalov-Naiditsch, Dortmund, 9.7.2005.

122. **18.Qd2! d×e3** (18...Nd5 19.B×d4) **19.Nb6+ ♔c7 20.Q×d8+! N×d8 21.Rd7+ ♔b8 22.R×d8+ ♔c7 23.Rd7+ ♔b8 24.R×b7++**. Apicella-Giffard, French Team Championship, 3.4.2003.

123. **25.Q×h5!! g×h5 26.Rg3+ ♔h8 27.Bg5! ♔g7 28.B×d8+ ♔f8 29.Bf6 h4 30.Rg7 Qb3??** (30...Qa4) **31.Rd2! Qc3 32.R×h7 ♔e8 33.Rd1 Qd4 34.Rh8+ ♔d7 35.R×a8 Bd5 (1–0)**. 36.Bb5+ Bc6 37.R×d4+ ♔c7 38.Bd8++. Andreikin - Riazantsev, European Individual Championship, Plovdiv, 27.4.2008.

124. **19...N×g3! 20.Rf3** (20.♔×g3 B×e5+ 21.♔f3 Qh4 22.♔e2 b4) **20...B×e5 21.Na×b5** (21.R×g3 b4) **21...Qh4! 22.e×f5 B×f5 23.Ra4 Be4!** (23...c4!! 24.♔g1 B×h3 25.R×c4 Q×c4 26.B×h3 Qh4 27.♔g2 Nh5!) **24.R×f8+?** (24.N×e4!) **24...R×f8 25.♔g1 Ne2+! 26.Q×e2 Qg3 27.Bf4 Q×f4 28.B×e4** (28.Bf3 Qg3+ 29.Qg2 Qe1+ 30.Qf1 Bh2+ 31.♔×h2 Q×f1 32.B×e4 Rf2+ 33.♔g3 Qg1+ 34.♔h4 Rf4++) **28...Qg3+ 29.♔h1 Rf1+ 30.Q×f1 Qh2++**. Van Wely-Timman, Wijk aan Zee, 13.1.2002.

125. **25.Rg8+! ♔c7** (25...N×g8 26.Qd6+) **26.Rf8 Rh7** (26...Rd7 27.Qh8; 26...Rg7 27.Na4 Q×d4

28.Qh8 Qd3+ 29.♔a1 Qe4 30.Rc8+ ♔d7 31.Nb6+) **27.Na4!! R×h6 28.Nb6 Qe4+** (28...Qh3 29.Re7+) **29.R×e4 (1–0)**. 29...Ra8 30.Re7+ Nd7 31.R×d7. Milov-Luther, Memorial Torre, Mérida, 15.12.2003.

126. **25.Q×b7!! N×b7 26.R×b7 ♔g8?** (26...c5 27.f3 Qc6 28.R×g7 ♔×g7 29.f×e4 Re8 30.e5 h6 31.Nf3 g5 32.Bd2 Qa6) **27.c5! h6 28.Bc4+ ♔h8 29.Be5! h×g5** (29...B×e5?? 30.Rh7++; 29...Q×e5? 30.Nf7+ ♔h7 31.N×e5) **30.B×g7+ ♔h7 31.Bf8+ ♔h8 32.Be7 Rb8 33.R×e4! (1–0). 33...f×e4** (33...R×b7 34.Bf6+ ♔h7 35.R×e8) 34.Bf6++. Kramnik-Topalov, Melody Amber (rapid), Nice, 20.3.2008.

127. **31.R×g7+! ♔×g7 32.Qb2!! Ba4** (32...Rf8 33.Bh4; 32...Rh8 33.Bh4 Qd8 34.b×c5 b×c5 35.Rb7 Rf8 36.B×h5!) **33.Rg3+ ♔f7 34.Rg5 Rf8 35.Bh4 B×d1 36.B×d1 Qd7 37.Q×f6+!! ♔×f6 38.B×h5 ♔e7 39.Rg7++**. Shengelia-Calistri, Cappelle-la-Grande, 15.2.2005.

128. **14.Q×e6+!! f×e6 15.N×e6 Qe5** (15...Qb6 16.N×g7+♔f8 17.Ne6+ ♔f7 18.N×c5+ ♔g6 19.Rd6!) **16.N×g7+ ♔f8 17.Ne6+ ♔f7** (17...♔e7 18.Rhe1) **18.Rhe1 Q×e1** (18...Q×h2 19.Nc5+ ♔g6 20.B×f6 Rhf8 21.N3e4 R×f6 22.N×f6 ♔×f6 23.N×b7) **19.N×c5+ ♔g6 20.R×e1 ♔×g5 21.N×b7 Nd4 22.Nd6 Rhf8 23.f3 b4 24.Nce4+ N×e4 25.R×e4** ...49 moves **(1–0)**. Ivanchuk-Karjakin, Melody Amber (rapid). Nice, 18.3.2008.

Bologan-Vaganian, European Club Cup, 12.10.2006.

112. **21.♘d5! e×d5** (21...♕d8 22.♘f6+!) **22.e×d5 ♖×c2 23.g6 h×g6** (23...f×g6 24.♕e6+ ♔f8 25.h×g6 ♗f6 26.g×h7) **24.h×g6 ♖f8 25.g×f7+ ♖×f7 26.♗×g7! ♖×g7 27.♕e6+ ♔h8** (27...♔f8 28.♖×g7!) **28.♖×g7! ♔×g7 29.♖g1+ (1-0).** 29...♔h7 30.♕g6+ ♔h8 31.♕h6++. Ivanchuk-Van Wely, Montecarlo (blindfold) 20.3.2006.

113. **25...♗f4! 26.♔f3 ♗e5! 27.♔×g4 ♖d3! 28.♖af1 f6! 29.♗f3 ♗d7+ 30.♔h4 h5 31.♖hg1 g5+ 32.♖×g5+** (32.♔×h5 ♔f7 y 33...♖h8++) **32...f×g5+ 33.♔×g5?** (33.♔×h5 ♗f4) **33...♔h7! 34.♘d5 ♖g8+ 35.♔h4 ♖×d5! (0-1).** 36.e×d5 ♗f6+ 37.♔×h5 ♗e8++. Esen-Golubev, Moscow (Aeroflot), 13.2.2006.

114. **21.♗×h7+! ♔×h7 22.♘e4 ♕e5 23.♖h4+ ♔g8 24.♗f4 d3** (24...♕d5 25.♗h6 f5 26.♗×g7 ♔×g7 27.♕h5; 24...♕b5 25.♕g4 f5 26.♕g6 f×e4 27.♕h7+ ♔f7 28.♗d6+) **25.♗×e5 d×e2 26.♘f6+! (1-0).** 26...♗×f6 27.♗×f6 e×f1♕+ 28.♔×f1, and mate on h8 follows. Short-Zhukova, Gibraltar, 28.1.2006.

115. **18.♖d×d5! ♗×d5** (18...♗d6, 18...♕c7) **19.♗a4+! ♔e7 20.♗c5+ ♔e6 21.e×d5+ ♔×f5 22.♗c2+ ♔g5 23.♕e3+ ♘f4 24.♕g3+ ♔h5 25.♗d1+ (1-0).** Langrock-Reddmann, Hamburg, 21.10.2001.

116. **23...♘f4+ 24.g×f4 ♕g6+ 25.♔h1 ♕h3+ 26.♖h2 ♕×h2+! 27.♔×h2 ♔f7! (0-1).** Then ...Rh8+. Neiksans - Stefansson, Liepaja, 1.8.2004.

117. **28.♗×h6!! ♖×f5** (28...g×h6 29.♕f4 ♖g5 30.♘d4) **29.g×f5 ♔h7** (29...g6 30.f×g6+; 29...♘c8 30.♖×g7+ ♔f8 31.♖g2+ ♔e8 32.♖g8+ ♔e7 33.f6+ ♘×f6 34.♖×c8 ♕×c8 35.♗g5) **30.♗×g7 ♖g8 31.♖fg1 ♕d8** (31...♘e5 32.h6 ♘f3 33.♖f1 ♘e5 34.♖g3) **32.♘d2 ♘c5** (32...♘f6 33.h6 ♕e7 34.e5! ♕×e5 35.♘f3 ♕×f5 36.♘g5+ ♔g6 37.♘e4+) **33.f6 ♕e8** (33...♖h8 34.♖g4 ♘d7 35.♘f3 ♘×f6 36.♘g5+ ♔×g7 37.♘e6+ ♔h6 38.♘×d8) **34.♖g6! (1-0).** 34...♖×g7 (34...f×g6 35.h×g6+ ♕×g6 36.♖h1+) 35.♖×g7+ ♔h8 36.h6 ♕d8 37.♖×f7. Motylev-Obolenskij, Kazán, 4.9.2005.

118. **30.♖×g6! ♖×g6 31.♗×c4 ♔e7 32.♖b7+ ♔d6 33.♕h5! ♗×c4 34.♘e4+! (1-0).** 34...f×e4 (34...♔d5 35.♕×f5++) 35.♕e5++. Beliavsky-Mamedyarov, Spanish Team Championship, 2.9.2005.

119. **20...♖×g2! 21.♔×g2 ♗×e4+ 22.♔h2** (22.♔g1 ♘f3+) **22...♘f3+ 23.♔g2** (23.♖×f3 ♗×f3 24.♘ac1 ♔d7) **23...♔d7 24.♖f2** (24.♖×f3 ♖g8+ 25.♔f2 ♗h4+) **24...♖g8+ 25.♔f1 ♗h4 26.♘×b4 d5! 27.♘×a6 ♖g1+!** (27...♕h2!? 28.♖×h2 ♘×h2++) **28.♘×g1 ♘g3+ (0-1).** 29.♔g2 ♘e1+ 30.♔h2 ♘f1++. Petkovski-Timoshenko, European Individual Championships, Ohrid, 1.6.2001.

120. **18.♘g6! f×g6?** (18...♖fe8 19.♘×e7+ ♖×e7 20.d×c5) **19.♕×e6+ ♔h8 20.h×g6! ♘g8 21.♗×h6! g×h6 22.♖×h6+! ♘×h6 23.♕×e7 ♘f7 24.g×f7! ♔g7** (24...♕b6 25.♕e5+ ♔h7 26.♖h1+) **25.♖d3 ♖d6** (25...♕b6 26.♖g3+ ♕g6 27.♖×g6+ ♔×g6 28.d5) **26.♖g3+ ♖g6 27.♕e5+ ♔×f7 28.♕f5+ ♖f6** (28...♔e7

29.♖e3+) **29.♕d7++**. Carlsen-Ernst, Wijk aan Zee, 24.1.2004.

121. **23.♘×e6!! f×e6 24.♕×e6 ♖d7** (24...♖d8 25.♖g3) **25.♖g3 ♕f8 26.♖e1! ♖aa7** (26...♖g7 27.♖×g7 ♔×g7 28.♕g4+ ♔h8 29.♕d4+ ♔g8 30.♕d5+) **27.♕f6+! (1–0)**. 27...♕×f6 28.♖e8+. Topalov-Naiditsch, Dortmund, 9.7.2005.

122. **18.♕d2! d×e3** (18...♘d5 19.♗×d4) **19.♘b6+ ♔c7 20.♕×d8+! ♘×d8 21.♖d7+ ♔b8 22.♖×d8+ ♔c7 23.♖d7+ ♔b8 24.♖×b7++**. Apicella-Giffard, French Team Championship, 3.4.2003.

123. **25.♕×h5!! g×h5 26.♖g3+ ♔h8 27.♗g5! ♔g7 28.♗×d8+ ♔f8 29.♗f6 h4 30.♖g7 ♕b3??** (30...♕a4) **31.♖d2! ♕c3 32.♖×h7 ♔e8 33.♖d1 ♕d4 34.♖h8+ ♔d7 35.♖×a8 ♗d5 (1–0)**. 36.♗b5+ ♗c6 37.♖×d4+ ♔c7 38.♗d8++. Andreikin - Riazantsev, European Individual Championship, Plovdiv, 27.4.2008.

124. **19...♘×g3! 20.♖f3** (20.♔×g3 ♗×e5+ 21.♔f3 ♕h4 22.♔e2 b4) **20...♗×e5 21.♘a×b5** (21.♖×g3 b4) **21...♕h4! 22.e×f5 ♗×f5 23.♖a4 ♗e4!** (23...c4!! 24.♔g1 ♗×h3 25.♖×c4 ♕×c4 26.♗×h3 ♕h4 27.♔g2 ♘h5!) **24.♖×f8+?** (24.♘×e4!) **24...♖×f8 25.♔g1 ♘e2+! 26.♕×e2 ♕g3 27.♗f4 ♕×f4 28.♗×e4** (28.♗f3 ♕g3+ 29.♔g2 ♕e1+ 30.♕f1 ♗h2+ 31.♔×h2 ♕×f1 32.♗×e4 ♖f2+ 33.♔g3 ♕g1+ 34.♔h4 ♖f4++) **28...♕g3+ 29.♔h1 ♖f1+ 30.♕×f1 ♕h2++**. Van Wely-Timman, Wijk aan Zee, 13.1.2002.

125. **25.♖g8+! ♔c7** (25...♘×g8 26.♕d6+) **26.♖f8 ♖h7** (26...♖d7 27.♕h8; 26...♖g7 27.♘a4 ♕×d4

28.♕h8 ♕d3+ 29.♔a1 ♕e4 30.♖c8+ ♔d7 31.♘b6+) **27.♘a4!! ♖×h6 28.♘b6 ♕e4+** (28...♕h3 29.♖e7+) **29.♖×e4 (1–0)**. 29...♖a8 30.♖e7+ ♘d7 31.♖×d7. Milov-Luther, Memorial Torre, Mérida, 15.12.2003.

126. **25.♕×b7!! ♘×b7 26.♖×b7 ♔g8?** (26...c5 27.f3 ♕c6 28.♖×g7 ♔×g7 29.f×e4 ♖e8 30.e5 h6 31.♘f3 g5 32.♗d2 ♕a6) **27.c5! h6 28.♗c4+ ♔h8 29.♗e5! h×g5** (29...♗×e5?? 30.♖h7++; 29...♕×e5? 30.♘f7+ ♔h7 31.♘×e5) **30.♗×g7+ ♔h7 31.♗f8+ ♔h8 32.♗e7 ♖b8 33.♖×e4! (1–0)**. 33...f×e4 (33...♖×b7 34.♗f6+ ♔h7 35.♖×e8) 34.♗f6++. Kramnik-Topalov, Melody Amber (rapid), Nice, 20.3.2008.

127. **31.♖×g7+! ♔×g7 32.♕b2!! ♗a4** (32...♖f8 33.♗h4; 32...♖h8 33.♗h4 ♕d8 34.b×c5 b×c5 35.♖b7 ♖f8 36.♗×h5!) **33.♖g3+ ♔f7 34.♖g5 ♖f8 35.♗h4 ♗×d1 36.♗×d1 ♕d7 37.♕×f6+!! ♔×f6 38.♗×h5 ♔e7 39.♖g7++**. Shengelia-Calistri, Cappelle-la-Grande, 15.2.2005.

128. **14.♕×e6+!! f×e6 15.♘×e6 ♕e5** (15...♕b6 16.♘×g7+♔f8 17.♘e6+ ♔f7 18.♘×c5+ ♔g6 19.♖d6!) **16.♘×g7+ ♔f8 17.♘e6+ ♔f7** (17...♔e7 18.♖he1) **18.♖he1 ♕×e1** (18...♕×h2 19.♘c5+ ♔g6 20.♗×f6 ♖hf8 21.♘3e4 ♖×f6 22.♘×f6 ♔×f6 23.♘×b7) **19.♘×c5+ ♔g6 20.♖×e1 ♔×g5 21.♘×b7 ♘d4 22.♘d6 ♖hf8 23.f3 b4 24.♘ce4+ ♘×e4 25.♖×e4** ...49 moves **(1–0)**. Ivanchuk-Karjakin, Melody Amber (rapid). Nice, 18.3.2008.